AFTER NORMALCY:
IN PURSUIT OF STABILITY

SELECTED POEMS
1997-2017

Poetry by
David F. Kirk

Riverhaven Books

www.RiverhavenBooks.com

AFTER NORMALCY: IN PURSUIT OF STABILITY is a compilation of work of the author's creation. Any similarity regarding incidents is entirely coincidental.

Published in the United States by Riverhaven Books,
www.RiverhavenBooks.com

ISBN: 978-1-937588-71-7

Printed in the United States of America

Edited and designed by
Stephanie Lynn Blackman
Whitman, MA

To my Mother and Father,
for encouraging me never to give up and
always to follow through on my dreams

CONTENTS

from *SANDCASTLE EMPIRES*

from *GHOST OF A BUTTERFLY*

from *RESPITE FROM REALITY*

from *THE EVOLVING DOOR*

from *CHALLENGED ON ALL FRONTS*

from *OVERLOOKING THE FROST*

from *SAFE DWELLING POSTS*

from *WINGS ON WORDS*

from *CALLIOPE OF VERSE*

from *WEATHERVANE OF CHANGE*

NEW POEMS

from *SANDCASTLE EMPIRES*

HIDE AND SEEK

Light-green apples, bruised & scattered,
upon the ground recovering from frost.
The nip and thrust of a lost tranquility,
even the fraud at the core of my being.

I longed for labor in fertile front yards,
desperately dreaming of peace & quiet.

To hear the snap from the cold-blooded wind,
like a piercing whistle through a mouthpiece.
The shrill recorder of gray-swept episodes
or storms belonging outside of scrapbooks.

I mourn the lifting of the fig leaf,
discreetly in place all these years.

Abrupt shift to a state of nakedness
covered in the gold-flaked orchards.
The posing with smiles for the camera,
even as an illness takes over like winter.

I am with you, under the tree of ripened regret,
unable to focus upon the fruit that hasn't fallen.

If only I could grow with the hint of sweetness,
from a solitary seed to a shared taste of success

to work to prevent the rotting
in a vast cemetery of my mind.

I will not let my soul be buried; I will not wither;
I will rise from under the weight of circumstance.

UNDER SUSPICION

The flattened demons, the smoked-out clouds
disappointing
in the direction of dead-locked experience.

I hear the voices; I hear the voices;
ill-tuned
like a guitar lacking the relevant string.

The inappropriate song, the whisper
devastating
like a compass of white-water regret.

I see through swollen eyes, vacant stares,
separated
like two isolated clumps of sea-grass.

The bittersweet opening to a better world
savoring
sunflowers growing old in middle-aged fields.

A WAKE

A caretaker arranges for the burial of Sanity.
Minds lowered to rest in antique-white wards,
where needle-thrusts achieve a Buddha-calm.

The staff laughs about patient self-awareness
as it checks every quarter-hour on the blood &
the pressured symptoms of checked-out minds.

Vacancies in rooms scrubbed clean of personality,
where blank faces cross into Emotion's morgue &
wait to be waked from a deep, blue-hazed slumber.

Awakened, like a pebble skipped across
the newly-rippled water of consciousness.

To yearn for Freedom, not the kind in textbooks,
but the sort you find in breathing in lilacs one day.

Far from the crypt of containment,
where people pass like sandpaper.

And, you feel the grit of being — exhumed from the dead.

VACANT STARES

The midnight ghosts from the West Coast deny the sunshine past, and
the night sky is haunted by a tombstone moon, overdosed on darkness.

The fleshed skeletons in the hall-closet are dragged, kicking & screaming,
into an emergency-room present, as shooting-stars are scared into silence.

The spider is scarred by the code-blue threat, an all-encompassing web,
and the associated wounds are frustrated by the restart of the madness.

The sadness, O the sadness, finds its way into the scrabbled night
where you have scribbled down the information without the insight.

Invisible & indivisible, a sinister thought arrives at another's doorstep,
where the peace that you sought lies buried in the cemetery on the hill.

The chains still cannot be seen, but they are heard,
and the rattle of memory forces you to the brink.

The dread slinks into your bones, and
you are unprepared for withdrawals.

The walking dead stare into the blank slate, with a blank look,
as bedsheets uncover a prayer that floats to a medium of hope.

The midnight ghosts aspire to unchain the past and
fly unencumbered into an ever-accepting sunshine,

where a wayward soul is determined to get its wings.

ABSENT-MINDED

To blank-out, to welcome
even the threat of thought.

Transmitters shut-down &
you feel so unconnected.

Sleep, the lotion of sleep,
on the dry skin of a mind
unable to think on its own.

Not a flake of thought, not an impulse,
not an urge, not a resistance to change,
only the horrible panic of nothingness.

The flat-lining of thought, the crisis —
the rear-view mirror totally obscured.

The inescapable breakdown, the calling out for help,
to cross borders from an accidental & complete void

to a recovery enabled under blankets of medications.
To warm up from a single inkling put-together
into an idea, until restored to the health of thought.

Not sure where you are going,
you desire to come back to joy,
transported again to a safe place,

calling, after all, upon the indispensable tow-truck of memory.

SURRENDER

The spectacle of losing your mind
round on carousels of irrationality,
riding up-and-down, so far down,
upon the saddle of an unstable horse.

To combat invasions of thought,
as if an outsider is at the reigns,
blinding & conquering Reason.

Overtaking back-channels of communication
with yourself, self-involved in stooped nights.

The white flag is flying.

The spectacle of losing your mind,
surrounded, compulsive cheeriness.
You spin out-of-control, dizzy lights,
overheard laughter & mass confusion.

Will it ever stop? Can you ever get off this ride?
To be overwhelmed by tear-stained revolutions
within yourself, a conveyor of homeless thoughts.

To need some peace and quiet from this detached reality —
to find yourself within reach of relief, with appeals to calm.

The merry-go-round is closed, though, until further notice.

COLLECTIONS

The knot is tied, and I cannot loosen the hold of love,
despite the homeless thoughts loitering in my mind.

I dwell upon the public benches within, preoccupied
with the parking of progress, the hoarding of sadness.

The past is cluttered with the relics of memory,
blank records & cold cases, after resolution.

Missing for twenty years, disappearing from the public eye,
I have been known to accumulate piles of bankrupt shadows.

The grating cadences of a long-lost paradise,
where I no longer possess comforts of home.

I have been dismissed, like that one last vagrant soul
who never returns the favor, pays back the kindness.

The knot is undone, and I resort to chasing ghosts,
who may not be recaptured in a self-serving world.

I track the unwanted souvenirs of loneliness.

HANDICAPPED

The crutches splinter into a million pieces, and
the unspeakable is swallowed: too many pills.

A preferred sparrow waits, tufted wings, tinged with violet:
why? Why does the arrow strike without backup support?

The voice is speckled with honor, consumed by choices,
savoring and wavering in a meadow of chocolate daisies.

The line goes dead; the take-out order is arranged; and,
the close-up danger is in the dosing, long after the fact.

The intervening ghosts rattle the meek, with impeccable timing,
as the incremental push is to drive past the tainted woodshed.

The last-second cry of sheep faintly could be heard, and
the shepherd is shunned for not tending & inspecting fields.

A shield feels a little feeble, and the pebbles are too small:
I would do anything to ease the flanked appeal of a falcon.

To prey upon gentleness, with back-handed compliments, and
a prompt refusal to apologize in the nature of a profiled hero.

The prescriptions for individual courage are measured,
and group therapy acts something like a miracle-cure.

One final chance is to blend the personal and the public:
a blur of healthy check-ups & a scourge of unhappiness.

A hundred years of mixed reviews: empty refills
and the bottled sensitivity to a radicalized dawn.

LOST IN THE PROCESSING

The rose-colored glasses, irretrievable,
like data on the other side of normalcy.

What once was had, forgotten,
in the frozen ponds of thought.

Waiting for the coming of another spring,
like geese having dropped out-of-sight.

Do you know what it is
like to lose a compass?

To be without direction, or
the aid of past appointments?

The coming & going
of obliged visitations?

He can't make it on time,
and the payments are late.

The vase is cracked and
even the laughter is forced.

Back to the drawing board,
to slow the inner dialogue.

Hearing cycles of self-chatter,
he yields this peculiar harvest.

In the red-coated fields, ripe with conspiracies,
he covets acceptance from an unknown enemy.

ON THE MEND

The bipolar world is approaching an end, parachutes,
and safe landings on the sandy beaches of normalcy.

A seagull has a damaged wing, overdue awakenings,
and the view from a day-room that doubled as a tomb.

I am better now, and the fog has lifted: from my window,
I spy an autumn bog with an embarrassment of cranberries.

To know enough to prove the doubters wrong, clouted doves,
who moved over the mowed-clover fields, fertile imaginations.

The bipolar world is tested by white-knuckled stress, fragile eggs,
and clear writing that enables me to present my best foot forward.

A nest is disturbed, and the little ones fly: a flurry of criticism,
and the direct assault upon the journey to a discernible Reason.

I am better now, and the fog has lifted: from my window,
I discover the sunbeam that seems to point to the rainbow.

A photographic-memory is triggered, beach-traffic, and
the epiphany that the broken ones have a shot at healing.

FLASHBACKS

A flurry of pictures scanned by
a man under internal demands,
where his lens is out of focus.

Institutional patient long past
the age of his coming of age.

Done in by wine-colored episodes.

Grasping for any exposure to Voice,
getting beyond a floor of negatives &
scuffling in dark rooms of thought.

Photographs of skeletons,
scraped of layered identity.

The appearance of bone.

In a corner, Reason, straight-jacketed,
unable to break free and improvise
in a domain of regimented impulses.

Blank stares, pill-boxes, &
clamped-down responses.

And yet never to bury the dream of a developed life.

LEFT OUT IN THE COLD

A mind like a skunk, disgruntled,
prowling in the weeds of thought.

It threatens to spray an unsuspecting world —
the crimes of instinct on cold-hearted nights.

An outcast, governed by fear,
resigned to the dark shadows.

Blackened and rabid thoughts,
without a spotlight of Reason.

No stopping the associations,
no relief in sight, I'm afraid.

The awful smell of worry &
the desperate need for help.

A mind, like that rabid skunk,
attempting to adapt to disease.

Too disturbed to protect itself &
too isolated for Nature's interventions.

The grass is dead, and the weeds thick;
nobody told me that life would be fair.

BATTLEFIELDS

The shrapnel undiscovered
beneath the skin of memory.

The undetected wounds
fester below the surface.

To heal what needs to be treated.

An Achilles' heel of unsubstantiated regret.

To hope for peace
in a lifetime of war.

These haunted dreams
open to interpretation,

where monsters escape in the dark,

and skeletons remain to remind us.

Invisible demons, once indomitable,
no longer able to inflict harm on us,

or conquer vulnerable enemies,
without the ammunition of rage.

Old wounds, hidden from view, still scare us into silence.

THE LIFE-PRESERVER

My affairs had been going quite well,
rather smoothly, like thin ice on a lake,
basking in the sun. Until a sinking
through crusted layers of instability.
In fact, I was issued a bitter shock.

It may have been better if
I had been wronged by another.
At least, I would have a party to blame,
a person to hold accountable.
Instead, I reach out to grasp — no one.

The questions well up like tears.
Is there any solace for imperial wounds?
Who will console the seemingly inconsolable?
Is there anything eternal but sorrow?
Will I be able to endure, like the blue spruce,
fortified against the cruelty of the coming winter?

The winter is upon me.

I am still, past frustrations, past illusions,
hanging on in a world of questionable truths.
I have lost my strength to complain
and am in the business of listening.
I hear your Word and am relieved.

My wishes, my sadness, my voice
seem to converge in my trust in you.
It is as if I am jumping into that lake in spring,
content to float, to wait, and to accept the waiting.
An eternity in the transcendent blue water,
immeasurable pools of grace.

HANGING ON

A man, at the mid-point of life, mysteriously adrift,
watches the fog roll in upon his well-crafted plans.

He stops to think & make his peace alone
in a rowboat on a lake in the mountains.

He smiles to himself. It is as if
the mountains anticipate his complaints
and say to him, "Why not you?"

Life is as it is — some paddle perpetually
against the currents, frustrated oarsmen,
while other passengers get a free ride.

His natural response is to curse the unfairness,
to reject the forces that threaten to pull him under.
He will not quit the fight to keep his head above water.

Over the edge of the boat, to the bottom of the lake,
he sees the muddied sediments & the mixed sentiments
that many feel in the underworld of sampled regret.

The private offer to persevere accepted,
he paddles home, with magical resolve
through the same fog we all may share.

The man may be out-of-work and unmarried,
still far from the shores of his expected bliss,
but he has committed himself to a bond with

the rest of the human enterprise and
the way it should carry out its affairs.

from *GHOST OF A BUTTERFLY*

VACATIONING FROM REALITY

Going through the motions without strong emotions
under brownstone caves, under a Mediterranean sky.

On a quick trip to the beaches of Portugal,
to forget the mind in the shade of thought.

Who could have guessed
the imminent dislocations?

A potent sun beats down upon me,
unshielded, burnt-skinned Reason.

My mind, previously so quiet, so efficient,
reserving a place as an assassin of analysis.

No longer living & dying like a shark,
feeding in the shallows of complacency.

My disciplined mind exposed in open water;
the crystal-clear thinking suddenly polluted.

To make sense out of nonsense,
a lonely enterprise in thought.

Hearing in my head the sound of drums,
and the vain attempts to stop the beating.

I have become undone like the onion
with peeled-back layers of confidence.

No longer can I cover up;
I have uncovered illness.

IN NEED OF REPAIR

Around a mountain, the color of emeralds,
up haunted paths of well-trafficked beauty,

I scramble past fast cars
in tracked lanes of thought.

Barely escaping, like the vampire
unable to take advantage of dawn.

Another day, a mind past dawn
with early indications of defeat.

An accident spirals out of control
as I put one step in front of another.

To quicken my pace, to outdistance thoughts:
a cross-country mind seen speeding downhill.

Someone over there in a well-groomed park,
hiding in the untidy recesses of imagination.

Is he after me? Will he get me?

Latching on to detective duty, clues
in apparent relationships of remembering.

To flag down facts in a pit-stop of evidence,
so sure that they pertained to me, only to me.

Keep it straight, trying to keep it straight,
and the faulty references keep coming.

Early signs of disconnected Reason.

VISIONS

From my bedroom window,
I witness armies of pigeons
making soft landings on roofs.

Birds put there, divinely arranged,
on the battlefield of a troubled brain,
craving order upon the receipt
of a sustained drive to madness.

The rain still pours down
in columns of military precision
onto my soaked plaid pajamas
as I race for spiritual intervention.

I swear I saw Jesus three times that early spring.
Once, on a crowded street, He glanced at me alone,
and I felt His compassion, became part of His bliss.

I swear I saw Jesus a second time,
climbing to the top of a small hill,
looking back at me with kindness
in a peaceful glow near to nightfall.

And yes, it is true, I saw Jesus a third time,
just around the corner from the blood bank,
where the Red Cross people shared his spirit.

A revolution, faithfully accepted in ordinary time,
but my mind tricks me into grasping at last straws &
embracing classic symptoms — delusions of grandeur.

As if Jesus would appear to me alone
in my private little zone of suffering!

A FINAL THOUGHT BEHIND THE THOUGHTS

Lying on his back on an emptied-out lawn,
paying loose attention to Memory's yawn,
remembering the open sigh of noon,
and then the closed whistle of defeat.

The nagging thought that
the stars are against him.

Glassy-eyed assumptions &
then the foggy conclusions,
if the outcome of his thoughts
yielded any such conclusions.

Circles, not pretty circles,
but circles circling circles until
he is worn down with an
ash-colored crayon of regret.

Some say take an aspirin or two
and that agitation will ease, go away,
like the villain at the end of a PG flick.

But he sees only the fault of
faulty patterns of the brain.

Making sense only to HIM. Uneasy wirings like
an OFF-THE-HOOK phone BUZZING in his EAR.
Starting from a truck parked in the dark outside his house

(just his luck!) then the Usual Suspects are out to get HIM.
Ah, where the HELL is the peace?
He wishes he knew; he wishes he knew —

OVERBOARD

The craft is leaking.

I am paddling toward an objective:
to rehabilitate a confessional style.

The current is moving me
in ways I never intended.

To reveal a secret.

I am less than
okay.
How about you?

Are you swimming
or
are you drowning?

The water is deeper than I thought.

BASIC STROKES

The virgin road, cleared of cumbersome deadwood,
promised copper pennies & diamond attachments.
I took the path unwittingly down to rough waters
where swift paddling & swifter currents led me from
a narrow river to a stunning vista of wide-open seas.

I had so long been flowing uninterrupted
down that American stream of mobility.
My own discipline in navy-blue territory
could not prevent breakdowns in craft.

Suddenly, out went power & glory
and in came the aspiration of
getting a clean-cut shave again.

Nurses then noticed:
clock stuck at noon.

Doggy-paddling.

PATIENT PROGRESS

Who among us wears the mark of the mentally ill?

We all are at risk, zeroing in on the target of
the brain and its disease, biology, & triggers.

The public generally wants to hear about
the antics of the few most deeply troubled.

They are paraded with a scotch-tape transparency
before prying eyes who see only danger & violence.

No concern for the individual who is shamed by
the collective imprint of extreme behavior.

A group, marginalized, is sized up as the enemy:
stigmatized, misrepresented, and then mistreated.

In the hospital, the visions & the visitors come to an end.
No one wants to be a part of what appears to be "abnormal."

The forms of medication wipe out the delusions at a cost
to patients who are cursed with a creative flatness.

To accept this compromised peace without vibrancy,
to negotiate the ultimate price — a structured compliance.

The affected reside on the safe side of sanity
with effective drugs & empathetic caregivers.

It seems that we all could win a long-term victory,
even as the inevitable losses add up along the way.

To preach a message that only experience can teach:
live as best we can, always on alert in a scary world.

DRIVING MAD

You could be that guy on the main street,
pacing and pacing and pacing and pacing,
talking to himself and talking to himself.

The Devil beats you down in the details:
eggshells crack in the back of the brain &
you hear the sustained voices that beg to be answered.

The choices are drained of significance
like the black eyes fighting for sanity
in the still wards of evaporated rewards.

The gash of memory & the gush of emotion:
you would do anything to rewind the clock.
Socks are put in an order only you understand.

The pills are taken off the shelf,
posters are plastered to the wall,
and you manage the hint of a smile.

All those miles registered with the hazard lights on:
full-scale efforts to drive toward a compacted style
even as you cannot silence those roadside demons.

All the while you see yourself
in the visions of that other guy
whose face goes blank & mood flat.

The last chance to rehabilitate the mind
where you are locked up in your room &
you own the notion of common property.

You and I could be that guy on the same street
as we intend to put an end to the threat of madness.

CONSTRAINTS

Through a cracked window, barred from normalcy,
a patient, forced to wear his disability on his sleeve,
looks out for the reassuring sight of lighthouses
along the jagged coastlines of a crooked world.

His perfect vision of the future has become blurred &
he cannot understand why the lights have gone out.

He paces the halls with a frantic urgency,
racing toward answers that will never come,
racking his brain about problems without solutions.

He puts up with the sharp slap of recognizable disdain
from nurses who get fed up with the cascade of babble
coming out of him in a dark, pressured stream.

"Everything will be okay," the staff members repeat
as they forbid razors and the freedom of movement
with the stated objective of protected compliance.

He feels in his bones the desire to be free:
to move beyond the addictions of the ward,
smoking away longevity, passing up time
with games of chance, without imminent meaning.

He occupies a space in which it is impossible to stand still.
A race past conformity on sleek, modern bicycles,
maneuvered by highly functioning cyclists who
ride too fast to worry about the least of their brothers.

The imperative to slow down, to adjust the mirrors,
and to reflect upon the flaws of a society where
privileges, both private & public, outshine rights.

OVERWHELMED

The masking tape is said to work wonders on a damaged mind.

The full-time exercises expressed like a weeping willow wilting
under pressure from an outside source that cannot be disclosed.

Delusions break the spirit. Jesus cannot be around the corner,
circling back to a discourse on the progress of the tormented.

We begin with genes and then the triggers of environment,
targeting the ones who see the FBI & CIA as co-conspirators.

The doors are pushed open and the thoughts rush through;
silence appears like a mask that will not diminish the fears.

I hear the loop in my thinking that returns me to a state of terror
as the weakened will ferrets out what can't make sense anymore.

To lose grip on the rational, like a boy unable to process
a world in which balls are flung at him indiscriminately.

At the margins, he is misrepresented as a troublemaker —
someone who is to blame for not wearing his illness well.

To be thought at fault is the introduction to mistreatment:
the hard-fought and overheated efforts to seem "normal."

Medications may restore the patient to coherency and
may stimulate a core noted for short-term improvement.

To imagine the soothing sound of the rain, until a downpour
& the disruption of inner peace expected by a compliant brain.

The control has left me afraid of overextending limits,
or, in a worst-case scenario, shutting down completely.

SAFE FOOTINGS

I spy a septic truck &
a news item on page ten
about mental health.

The ground is solid this Christmas season,
like a troubled mind firmly held in check
before bubbling up & breaking through.

The local clinic is closed for the holidays,
and I can't register my worries about you.

We were so close
to being rescued.

I dug up the remains of yesterday.

ON YOUR OWN

The glue that holds together the good news, feathered repercussions,
and the brain disease that eats away at the semblance of normalcy.

Balance has been disturbed in the otherwise tranquil suburbs
where you get your fill of the stuff from the staff kept at home.

To comb the neighborhoods with the glut & rust
as the rot surfaces on the patrol borders of sanity.

Beetles flee the scene of the crime
as first-responders cannot believe.

There is no relief in sight, still breathing,
like a lion in fantasy after the artful light.

To barter with those who have gone before
through the door to a darker place of unrest.

The best of times collapse at a roadblock
where you are afraid to admit to treatment.

The meat of the argument is held back:
fat is removed from the shadowed bone.

To lean on sane spirits on your shoulder
where you can't repay them soon enough.

The fuss is over the medium — converted skeptics
who feel the presence of what cannot be explained.

The drain is plugged; the plumber is occupied;
you are sure that you can fix the leak yourself.

All is not well, though, in the meadows of the mind.

EXPOSED

The refreshing thing lingers beneath the rock & the hard place:
refurbished dreams star in a play in which the toad takes a bow.

To show the other side the purposes that make them cringe,
the difficulty is to binge and to be able to execute the dance.

The toll is registered in fancy notes that appear to move well:
the harp soothes the sick in fearful, suspended waiting rooms.

I take this opportunity to connect with the unconnected:
we have to traffic in stained letters, in a backlog of tears.

The train almost comes off the track; accidents multiply and
we reach beyond the melancholy to seek the bubbles of grace.

To force ourselves to cover over the pain, doing no harm
in the nature of fig leaves modestly addressed, wounded.

To make the rounds with a hidden shock of rooted sadness,
mocked by the modern and its display of roosters at dawn.

The light has violated the stump speech of regret,
and I pick up the last chance to deliver this hope.

No more moping in the doctor's office of illness,
talking to ourselves as if we could find the cures.

The allure of a healthy life is almost within grasp;
we try to extend with bayonet-surges, final gasps.

To winterize the prospects and to update the existence,
a coveted trophy may rest on the mantle of self-esteem.

The letting go, though, is what ultimately sets us free.

ON THE WAY

The argument for sanity first was made in the age of fossils
as the stage was set for an intervention of modern influences.

To waste away your talents in a foreign land
where a bold world was initiated with a bang.

To be a part of history and a nightmarish past
as parishes of the sick ended with a whimper.

A new age of patients is observed out of place
on the Pacific Front where internal wars are waged.

Their notion of free speech frustrates the point of brevity
as they engage in extended sessions of excessive chatter.

All will not end well within the boiling cauldron of the mind
as a dragon flails its wings in a weird contortion of confusion.

Be wary of the cinnamon-flavored breath of the beast
who won't shut up in the fiery climate before sunset.

The metaphor of the mirror reflects a dark temperament
as the sorcerer shatters the glass in a light white room.

Critters in the cold are noticed with sated bellies, but
the Satan stuck in the mind has no such satisfaction.

The tactful gift is the rational response
even as the knight falls upon the sword.

To report a delusional stream of thought
without the potion or the pills to be saved.

The ill-timed attempt to right a persistent wrong.

OPEN TO HELP

The therapeutic approach is paired with the prescription drugs:
an advocate is tempered by the drip-drip of the pouring rain
in a change of venue, in a totally new format, positive impact.

I am making up for the time in which only the good shined.
Who am I to categorize the broken wing of a feathered bird?
The burdens shift to the deferred calls of a challenged referee.

I wait up for the moment when the butterfly is taking flight;
it is beautiful through the eyes of someone who charters life,
who barters love for love, and won't seek anything else in return.

I reach out for your hand, each touch confirming the support,
firmly grasped like someone who was thrown a final lifeline.
The grind is to find a way in the cell phone world of gray mist.

"I insist, I insist," said the pauper to the prince. You are too old
to compromise in the portal to the past. The pills are necessary.
The record is complete enough with appropriate levels of sleep.

And I cannot forget the stress management, breaking points,
and peaks & valleys in a fallible place as fingers are crossed.
Face to face in a crazy world, the cruel occupy a lonely space.

Nonetheless, a spotted butterfly is taking flight; it is beautiful.

from *RESPITE FROM REALITY*

WITH GOOD BEHAVIOR

To accept the carpet ride to a halfway house: dandelions & pine needles
as nine chipmunks could not get out of a funk in a scramble for meaning.

The preamble to our independence is scripted on paved walkways
as genies are un-bottled & blotted out on paid administrative leave.

To wish for a dose of fresh air happiness that does anything
but eradicate thinking & feeling with a nice bedside manner.

The abiding passion that you and I pursue is shelved:
cases fraught with danger to the bastion of the brain.

To refrain from casting aspersions upon what we don't comprehend:
a friend is the predicate for the weak link that leans on our sorrow.

A day pass is issued; pillars of the community are quick to exit;
we lose track of the steel restraints imposed before release.

A pint of Vanilla Heath Bar Crunch is freely given and freely received
as the spiritual connection to nourishment is stalked in the main lobby.

Departures, though, always leave behind an essential part of us.

GET AWAY

A sanctuary is actually elevated, atmospheric pressure
with the dated vestiges of an invasive stigma, uncured.

To dig into surefire demurrals, into the rocky confidence
as a mockingbird keeps a straight face in the wake of fate.

A silver lining is baked into a marbled cake,
but no one knew just how far away you were.

To burn through the cash, to discern the secret battle:
the loved ones are saddled with what they cannot fix.

A journey sticks to the basics — health and happiness —
as antelopes ailing with fear elope near the water's edge.

To coax the reluctant ones off the edge: coughs of relief
as a positive attitude takes place in the case of subsidies.

A sanctuary is ultimately earned, retired rocking chairs
where the rare footage is released in the public venues.

Pending full disclosures, you assume the brand and
absorb the blame after the imagined & real ridicule.

To be worn out even in the opening phases of conflict.

REVITALIZED

The cobwebs hang in the madhouse and in other decrepit institutions
with a creeping suspicion that all will not end well, guttural contempt.

To cut the sheets until they fit the mask of insanity: shielded faces
under phantom-white ceilings streaked with a feel of real isolation.

The prior authorization takes time, and a dose is dispensed like a eulogy
that arrives at a strange habitat way too late, even too late for repentance.

To facilitate any form of concentrated therapy like electric shock
with facile dismissals locked into the DNA of uninformed skeptics.

Due diligence is conducted by those with nothing to lose, and
everything to gain strains of coagulated Reason left out to dry.

To lie like a cantaloupe in an open field waiting to become ripe,
waiting for any eager parties to identify a type of firm acceptance.

The terms of art are copied with invisible ink, powers of suggestion,
and hypnotic appeal from someone who can't tell exactly where he is.

Hell is anywhere and everywhere, separated from the font of love
who courts the good side of our natures, who guides the best of us.

We bus the trays & waiter the fruit of knowledge for eternity, uncertain
until the staff has done its job to replenish our lives toward better health.

To be of sound mind is the gift of restoration
as that clarity of thought is icing on the cake.

LOST LYRICS

The tree toads album the silver lining
with a tumult of bloated extravagance.

They pay lip service to a body of work,
like two peas in a pod, quirks of destiny.

An entire universe is voided
out of paranoid expectations.

To annoy the dire firestorm of the cursed,
nursed from the milk of tense renditions.

I don't know the words, but I have heard the song.
In the conquered evening, tree toads are received.

The singers of parody flourish in the wetlands
as they let go of the tunes, serenading the moon.

To gnaw away at the semblance of normalcy
in the stored valor & recompense evermore.

The heavens open at a light touch we really feel
as the safety gates gleefully invite us back home.

To triumph over worry after indictments of Reason:
rabid thoughts are spied after false charges of treason.

The lost & found are naturally recovered like mature myrtle
spreading over the ground after anthems to vacuum the sky.

UNRESOLVED

A collective amnesia fabricates the calm: placated placards
with punctuation marks that poster the raw monster's brow.

To row, row, row your boat: routine songs suit the wronged
on the precipice so far from the rustle of healthy fall leaves.

A "Yes-man" thrives on common ground, ancient regimes, and
a siege that only unfamiliar egrets carry with them regrettably.

To quilt together the patches that march the memorial protests
on an advocate's timetable and on a nickel & dime program.

A selective appreciation dampens the yawn with a handkerchief
as emotion stirs up old memories with a nod to the hijacked dawn.

To stack the weakest link atop a strong base without boundaries:
a cough elevates the discussion to nurse a tiny yelp for assistance.

The help appears to metaphor our shuttered house for the time being
as ties bind us together and divert us from a sudden break in reality.

To pity the soul jeopardized by the quick slant to compact language
in a slick business to recant what we cannot accept, in boldfaced hurt.

A mosquito draws blood on a canvas chosen only by him.

RELAPSED

The ghosts recognize the ward under the guise of makeshift woe:
to go back, to retreat with mini-shakes in plain vanilla confidence.

To ensure the administrator & staff offer a life raft to rival the Devil,
who won't give up the mind games that grind and maim the present.

The way out appears to be a well-vented track as pills are swallowed
and the body & brain are invaded by a stupor, as dirty laundry is aired.

To excuse the compliant dream that screams with a restrained drama:
the house that dislodges secrets is on the outside of a perimeter of fear.

The settled scenario is like a walk to a place that may never be known:
the other has no idea of the internalized pain & the penalized honesty.

To obsess upon the ghosts and the haunted pasts of passive mourning:
an escape is made through trial & error efforts to repair and restore us.

OUT OF ORDER

Experience fevers the scarlet letter, blotches of Good,
as a continuance, are botched before the rainbow's step.

Nuisances obviously weep for a black & white insanity
coded in a heinous corner where goats scope corpses.

The poor devil didn't stand a chance, pandering in a park
where carrier pigeons fidget a message of utter nonsense.

The address isn't known, and the bottles aren't redeemed,
as fear is coddled and condoned in the toddler's formula.

The flat is exposed close to outrageous hazards
where a black taxi synchronizes the Twinkie sky.

The crinkle-cut fries reprise one last meal
where the scheme is perverted in meaning.

An office view is excluded from the Northern Lights
as a backseat driver beats up & sacks the purple haze.

Nothing fits. The snow goose goes & snoozes
until it's too late to wake up even the informed.

To fake the normalcy with malcontents in the attic
where the emphatic pause is caused by experience.

A scarlet letter marks pain that the audience can't see
as the laurels are crowded with a personal vindication.

ROUTINE FULFILLMENTS

A cheap coffee pot is brewing on a blue-spotted morning
where cornflakes are anything but plain fodder for thought.

I feign the favors that contribute to refusals
on a writer's block, on a midnight's clock.

The past did not return from storm warnings
after the blackout that demolished memory.

I ditch the hint of pretense by all accounts
with an accent scented by lavender vendors.

The doors open to the internal headquarters
where a person self-medicates on his own.

I am alone. The sedatives defer the chill, and
a pioneer auditions a legacy through negatives.

The capability is broadcasted and fueled for all to see
as the trail is blazed over a bridge, a frail span of fate.

I relay the frantic tributes with a semblance of respect
and the equal treatment that friends our intrinsic worth.

A tailspin is corrected even in a hungry artist's studio
where the tongue projects a flight of words within view.

I begin yet another morning doing what I love
in the common areas that knock down barriers

and connect the dots for the "haves" and "have-nots."

GRATEFUL REFLECTIONS

A tragic fabric knits together the indispensable ones
as a tense standoff is averted by an astute specialist.

To refute the chrome-gray trouble, the empty pill bottles,
and homegrown liquor prohibited under the outlaw sky.

Youth grimaces for what it cannot take back
after scoffing at pitfalls that only tag another.

A lesson is learned; optimism is outgrown:
the hospital nurtures the privileged to laugh.

And yet we cry, even the guys hidden beneath uniforms
with frazzled appearances that commonly cut to the quick.

Youth crickets the absolutions that wash & batter hope
in the lineup that intimidates only after riding the pine.

Sometimes the wise suffer the orange rind and
range over territory generally reserved for stars.

To stitch the fabric enough to make it complete:
a nightclub is deleted from a standup memory.

The running joke chokes on what has come to pass
on the treadmill and even on the offramp of a life.

A specialist is good at straightening the curves or
at least riding out the swerves that rhyme Reason.

To love the interlocked fingers of fate
that we notice, inherit, and aim to control.

In the post-normal world, we are chosen to avoid the nightcap,
accept the nap, and embrace the apps that espouse moderation.

To be ever thankful for earned insight, poignant memories & moments,
that only an individual can access in the process of acute remembering.

WITHDRAWN

Embarrassment stalks the harassed after hours,
after cogent claims so remote from grandiosity.

To hand over power from those who pander and cower:
you will anchor mini-miracles in the rancor of evasions.

The occasional lyrics won't diminish the force of your song,
executed as if a romance was paused under the shut window.

To donate the essence of spirit & dance, and to salvage grace
as the white knight is lost like the bank clerk's deposit slips.

The cause of concern depends upon the clandestine mission and
the sly additions to a humdrum logic, counting chickens & sheep.

To cheapen the accountant's ledger of Good & Evil, grieving,
as premonitions put the ones you love in the way of a nemesis.

A visceral feeling in the gut gets all the attention,
but you restrict your reaction to replay the facts

in a storyline that pleads for immediate interventions.

ABSENT

The student shops at the EZ-mart for a carton of skim milk:
alienation is heard in his timid voice with silk-like imitations.

To portray the psyche, fractured eggshells and crack-houses,
where the fragile are addicted to what they cannot sustain.

The student refrains from calibrating his sixth sense:
he rents out a studio, Buddha, and a spiritual void.

To annoy the teacher who won't stand for misconduct:
she hears textbook excuses that he flaunts in homeroom.

The student who roams the familiar haunts cannot be safe
as his recurring dream conspires to eliminate his ease.

To legalize the pot and mesmerize the valedictory speech
as illness graduates on to the next stage of his many faults.

The student is halted, interrupted farewells,
as he is aware of the abduction of Reason.

To luck out and to benefit from outreach
that's in the best interest of the missing child.

CALLING OUT

To pace back and forth with a trace of simulated regret and
to let down the ambitious bounds of sponsored reassurances.

I am fine. Or so says the serpent who whispers in my ear.
The hiss is of loss, and the river panics in its overflow duty.

To flower in the gutters and to flutter in the dressing gowns:
I play billiards in my sleep; the guess is in the corner pocket.

I am lucky enough. Multiple meanings go by the board,
and a horror show affords one last opportunity to scream.

To regulate the dry humor in a footnote, taking its place
in the tragic negativity, placating vociferous capitulations.

I am losing my footing. Comfort food mashes tolerance,
and leather boots are a bear to get on even in fair weather.

Feedback. Facts breed opinions; snowbirds head south;
and their offspring scoff at supper in the late afternoons.

I am worn out. No one cares that the clock has stopped,
and the thick stacks of op-ed columns no longer satisfy.

The current status is of a giant in crisis
under the thumb of an oppressive night.

SUBDUED

The projector keeps highlighting the affected areas of harm:
memory sacrificed by accidental powers, recorded wounds.

To make the rounds with controlled tempers, manic trembling:
the brain is the nonstop store to outsource the working Devil.

The myths lurk in the ungodly recesses of a stiff necessity:
I soldier on the battlefield as life is flattened & sealed shut.

To yield to the terrible dilemma in the crucible of lemons,
where taste goes sour and the hours are pasted on the wall.

A prince falls in a flash upon the sword, latter-day warriors
who are in constant contact with a voice from another world.

To unveil the choice to expose the rattling in the mind:
I confine the chatter as pigeons feed on inconsistencies.

A vision is too much to witness in rocking chairs
where the scene is rarely as composed as it appears.

To close the book on a viper & a sloth
who won't settle for a negative answer.

An affirmative reply is tucked under the covers
where sleep is the best way to quiet the demons.

from THE EVOLVING DOOR

David F. Kirk

HAUNTED

The scissors are exorcised in a black mass, in a cat's cradle
where a sharp needle's wrath penetrates the litter of blades.

To obliterate the usual Kit Kat Halloween, spindles of spook:
a blue light pilots the raven who sees the horror show in 3D.

Shards of glass bleed the body, and a how-to manual operates well
within the shambles of a loose connection to pilfer the testimonials.

To pester the moan that accompanies the dark side of the murky mind:
a candle is identified in a homeless shelter where ghosts have a home.

A big heart is heard in a herald's obituary: the actual is acutely recalled
as the artificial pump gives out, and he is backed into a corner naturally.

To patter the feet in a troop of costumed pallor, pajamas in neon light:
a night sky is lit up by a procession of ghouls who congest the traffic.

The emphatic response is to spell out the monsters, sponsored
in a reclusive retreat as Hell is definitely more trick than treat.

UNEARTHED

The snow frowns upon a release into the unbalanced life
where a hard freeze is contemplated without a safety net.

To fret & fritter away the good name stenciled on your back:
a frenzy is streamed like a grand bargain grooved & stacked.

Gravity takes care of the grapefruit with common sense frost,
with the summons to appear before the exhausted magistrate.

To graduate: a cost/benefit analysis, theorems worn in thermals
as the bones are too cold to foster a consideration of the unborn.

The rose has thorns that cannot live, rotting in a vase
until the temperature is raised to the point of a great awakening.

To take a chance on the next best thing: a test of patience shivers,
and a discovery is planted in the open fields that fail the orchard.

A shallow grave is like a harvested narrative
where the meaning lies just below the surface.

DAMAGED

The dam broke, and I spoke out against the famished heart.

To depart from the playbook with uncompensated stars
who are hardwired to conspire with the specter of floods.

The docile gutter the affected zones of the hungry bones.

I am wiped out among the stone-faced vipers
who sting with venom then go their own way.

The naysayers in the waiting room are hard-pressed to believe
on leave from the West Coast sun where the upbeat host is done,

before water is poisoned under the weakened bridge.

I am poised to be that patient at the alma mater of fear
where my legacy is overwhelmed and severely spoiled.

A martyr disables suspicion, recoiling from a dust bowl

and creeping into the mystery of an un-welcomed flood
as the broad sweep of stimuli annihilates a broken brain.

I am painfully aware of the ordeal, zealously guarded

as walls are downed, and the protected are vulnerable.
In the aftermath of the scare, I master the next chapter.

UNSETTLED GROUNDS

To shy away from conflict, the chameleon shifts his position
in fitting rooms where he accepts whatever is handed to him.

The fuming ones are written into the fault lines; earthquakes
and the forsaken are worth more than the star broadcaster live.

To bribe the chief of operations, who is satisfied with a silent majority
in the sad aftermath of a riot meant to voice deep-seated claims.

The frustrations are deeded from the original owners of property
as the recipient earns a demonstration without a gifted tomorrow.

To waver before the demons who keep the puzzle from completion:
a complaint is buzzing in a plaintiff's ear, painted in zero tolerance.

A resolution is coming down the pike, whatever the psychic stance or
the straddled ignorance: the outcome will seep into our consciousness.

To weep for the staunchest allies or enemies aligned on opposite sides:
a tragedy is buried on the front page. Conventional wisdom, I'm afraid.

NEVER LOOKING BACK

The burnout is admitted
    with bad bouts from a delicate brain
as the turn of the main emergency switch
    goes off in the dark.

To jar the senses in common rooms of shampoo & potential:
I am positively sad about prior restraints on future prospects.

The reaction is mixed:
    a cold slice of pepperoni pizza sits out, and
the slick banter of innocence
    is kept quiet in sold-out reputations.

To sicken the body and to poison the mind as separate stories are told,
as memory is unable to repair the most basic forms of shared emotion.

The show is readily available for pickup
    even as the front door is shut, and
I am happy to enter the structure,
    waiting to dislodge nostalgia in my throat.

To dote on the nonrefundable message,
    fables that cannot be taken back:
the glow from the desk is never too late
    to illuminate the heart of caring.

A scare is averted in the narrow escape
    from self-imposed blockades and
scathing reviews that have no place
    in a feud over the terror of reunions.

I will connect with you despite the stigma that spatters our very being:
my stratified soul may rage in a civil war, but I extend my hand in love.

A lightbulb moment shines in our reconnected lives
where it is never necessary to pass along a final sorry.

TUNED OUT

The radio is playing static, and I cannot stop the misfiring of neurons
as two actors admire each other in the hardwired imbalance of music.

To imbue them with the applicable greeting card defense:
        a get well wish
with a rule that only the lonely will tackle a textbook
        execution of a case.

The criminally insane flatter the Penguin
        in war zones as a czar won't lie
on the stand, and the last known witness
        talks with excitement to his boss.

To traumatize the loss as the walking wounded
        are impaired of judgment:
they hit the sauce and trigger the psychosis
        that lands them in the slammer.

A hammer crushes the nail:
        even carpenters hear the racket in their heads, and
the noise is too much for anyone else
        coping with a profound breakdown.

The radio is still playing static,
        and I don't know where to assign blame
in a characteristic song that rhymes recovery
        and the belongings of love.

In an anonymous cell, an overactive brain
        compensates for pervasive change,
and my own medley of music evades
        a creepy rendition of irreversible errors.

UNDER INVESTIGATION

To decipher the clues that flew over the madman's resolution,
      flasks of whiskey:
a pocketknife is banned from the premises after a knock
      at the door of ignorance.

Knowledge is fully employed at the halfway house
      where insight is but a fraud:
he is nodding off on a detective's watch
      as he figures out the discord of invective.

To go back to the elective procedure:
      electric shock therapy mellows a mood,
and the shell of a prudent patient is cracked
      as the other drives himself nuts.

The words are strung out on the tongue's grid
      with what the group held in —
in confidence, the stuttered ones hinge
      on the sanitized reception of thought.

A sleuth follows the trail to a safe harbor of sanity,
      under surveillance
as a haven is sufficient to crowd secrets
      in an acknowledged safe place.

An insatiable appetite is to recapture the playful side
      of a wide-eyed child:
no one is programmed to go off his meds
      in an unpredictable compliance.

The defiant ones cripple the comfort that comes
      with the territory
in a buried plot where a protagonist rots & rises
      to decode the sky.

CONFRONTING THE WILDERNESS

The dysfunction occurs at the junction of juvenile & adult distress:
a cult of grown tigers is soothed and stressed at the breaking point.

To embroil ourselves in an opaque sadness: sweet & sour relevance
in the smart talk as we are trained to breed fear through caged eyes.

The push & shove mentality is shoveled out of the conscious mind:
a park is marked by a fatal attraction to the fullness of imagination.

To capture the unrestrained influences and turn them into solid gold
in rapt attention to detail where a crisis retains an element of danger.

A whole course in human nature is our sustained guide:
        a jungle of delegates
               as we try to tame the wild beast within us,
                   with jaded trust in a mild zookeeper.

GONE AWAY

The American citizen bitters the condescending logic:
a family of four modulates from a mad dash to Reason.

To pretend all is well with pelicans on the beach,
and a peach tree discovered in the pit of a dream.

The drips of dew drops condense on a white rose
where our woes are dyed with a permanent stain.

To feel your pain discerned from the surface of a curfew
as the dark regions substitute for the whole destitute heart.

Sarcasm is the cover for the waiting pool in transition
where the prompt response is to embrace the snowbirds.

To disturb the gift horse in the mouth of the South
as a ration of national remorse is exhaled in a breath,

in the death of a frail goodbye to irrational gratitude.

IN A DARK PLACE

The blank page beckons in the blackness of madness:
a blade switches on & off in the kitchen swan song.

To cough up the remainder of a holiday candy cane
in the candid exposure that rains on the sweet parade.

The model is broken, and the writer repeats himself again
as he fades into sunset where the burn is too much to take.

To make good on a promise: he touches on raw feelings and
consummates a deal that would solace the inconsolable.

The wounds can't be abolished under a lunatic's supervision
where he is in no position to group the alphabet soup of despair.

To letter the love and to bare the needy soul:
a watch is set to stop on another's timetable.

Timing is not right, though, and rhyming is in debt to reticence
where the hands of the clock are moved to chime stable ground.

BEYOND THE GRAVE

To ruminate on the tombstone cratered in another world
as the corporeal loses its flesh that a stork had delivered.

Quivers of desire and choirs in the river of doubt
where the lush ones are pushed out one last time.

To task the quick & easy: Reason evaporates
as milk spoils too soon in the ruins of a raid.

The buffoon dies after he buys another vowel,
in the Wheel of Fortune, in a staple of articulated love.

A free spirit is shaped starting from nothing
in the irrational faith in the substantive ghost.

On the cusp of supposed trust,
he leaps to conquer the rancor

that bandits the unsuspecting moon.

DIMINISHED STATUS

Therapy eases us into a self-proclaimed sadness:
a thought withers on the vine privy to profanity
that winds up as the bane of our pithy existence.

To distance the collar from the chain-link fence:
a consequence frolics in the alcoholic's playpen
as plenty of straight arrows pay for themselves.

A witching-hour sentiment leaves us in the doghouse,
and the potion is proportionate to the lousy chamber
where the magic is too lame to bedazzle anyone else.

The mundane are frazzled in hour-long sessions
recorded for posterity as our sanity is smuggled:
tricks we play ourselves are swept under the rug.

To chicken out with a noncommittal attitude
that fits the ironclad ambivalence of restraints
in radical claims to let go of a talker on a ward.

To walk the path not taken: apparitions listen
to the shrinking violets coughing up violence,
chalked up to experience as the lights go out.

ADVERSE REACTIONS

In the bowels of another low-class Evil fully vilified,
I declassify a vowel in a constant procession of letters.

To swim in an alphabet soup without fixed coordinates
until the game is scrabbled in a corroborated standstill.

The allegations are out in the open, coping with a criminal concept,
with a CIA conspiracy theory until words reflect paranoid subjects.

To void the excesses of sects and cults without insults:
I am afraid of immediate evasions & short-term denials.

An empty vial is on the dresser: vested interests and
the emergence of an exception to muster a strong love.

from *CHALLENGED ON ALL FRONTS*

MINDFULLY CHALLENGED

To stigmatize the reluctant patient inducted lately into infamy:
a symphony of noise is poised to overtake the vacant backdrop.

The stop & go traffic in the mind is trying to find a resting place
as the police pledge to hold up the race to internalize a crackup.

To pack & unpack in the vast territory within: a cry is heard, and
the wolves circle until the story of terror is told in an instant flash.

The stash of memories is pressured under the weight of secrets
as a weekend is predicated upon a chance to collect its thoughts.

A nagging suspicion lags behind an upfront visit to calm the nerves:
knowledge slips the curve as stigma sounds like the clash of titans.

Titans drown out the reluctant patient who still fights for relevance
in an overstimulated world as a clock is alarmed by its own passing.

GOING ALONG

True disability is filled with caveats and "what ifs":
a different piece of destiny is buttered on burnt toast.

To turn the boast into a slice of humble pie:
tumult hides under a surface of flaked calm.

The security fakes homage to the hurried demons
who devastate the vast sequence of Good & Evil.

To grieve fully for what could have been found:
an iceberg of tears melts a temporary hardship.

A star is born, and a storm is barred from normalcy
as ordinary members take flight in chronic disrepair.

TAINTED

To specify the question "why" that funnels daybreak:
a braid of locks and the wistful return
to the golden goose who fabricates a dose of nonsense.

Dense materials of youth are spattered like egg yolks
in a farewell spoof as shells are compromised
by a dawn of feigned interest from fake spies.

To file a secret report as documented co-conspirators
raid authenticity: we lament the cough
from an urban legend — cheating, lying, & stealing.

A wheel goes full circle: a child leaks word
that sharks are out of the tank, & chosen seagulls
have an appetite for random discourses on static fate.

A noise churns like butter: old-fashioned precedent
& dysfunctional serum as the truth is post-rational,
growing up with a surge of nostalgic rumors.

BUILDING UP

Exhibitions of self-control, second-class souls, and
cast-iron cauldrons that cannot solve the mystery.

To clatter beneath the acute history of hysteria:
a statistic shutters under the committee's glare.

The sharing is done: a meekness shuns the weakness
as a minor threat snowballs into a collective call to arms.

To better the codependent karma:
a last stand is finally grandfathered.

A cockpit madness, admissions mock the sane response
in a dangerous concert of sustained, orchestrated disgust.

CHARGED

Good intentions pivot upon a giving tree:
a crime is enabled by a credible zealot.

To convict the jealous of a lone wolf betrayal
in common areas that won't lull him to sleep.

A proactive leap is enough to slow the demons
who seem to dominate the trigger-happy world.

To trap the universal tune within a particular venue:
a heart is immune to a pending bout with madness.

A song matters even in the gray regions of doubt
as a siege is about a resort to a troubled Reason.

Treason, treason, the mission is incomplete
from a meeting place of the disgraced mind.

A diagnosis of a grave threat misses the mark, and
he is saved from a mob, barking up the wrong tree.

HELD CAPTIVE

The stimuli were processed, prim & proper melancholy
until the steadfast became unwound in the breakdown.

To brown-nose a day trip on secure hospital grounds:
a brittle assessment was relative to the roster of rules.

The one-way communication attended to the lifesaver
as trust was bought with lip service to an abused Truth.

To trip upon the front step to an arts & crafts playroom:
glitter was sprinkled atop crayon marks, green with envy.

An awkward moment was created by a mean supervisor
who sprayed a cannon of wrongs from a canon of words.

To imagine an opening day lineup in the padded space
where a ballgame broke the barriers to a regulated world.

A diagnosis begs the question: what difference does it make?
The schedule is analyzed like the infield grass — open to errors.

RUINED

To flash indications of indignation: a national amnesia
where the disease overwhelms the physical evidence.

The mind is fragile, and the magic is naturally visible:
a hero develops a complex with an aptitude for pride.

To prove the case in point beyond a reasonable doubt,
he anoints himself as pure despite the despot within.

The trial occurs at the best spot for a functioning system:
a man chronicles a fading light he wishes he couldn't recall.

To have had it all and to have lost touch with plush reality:
the influx of draconian measures and the very public guilt.

A pill can't absolve the Devil: stone-faced indifference and
the submissions to a headliner in persuasive disconnect.

TRICKLE DOWN

The monotony is in the wishful thinking: thick slabs of hope
and the slippery slope that dabbles in a bittersweet attitude.

Never to skip a beat and to optimize the existing options
on a continuum specializing in the bountiful range of rain.

The drizzle and downpour are bound to dampen his mood
even as the pampered is new to the business of drowning.

To pound the dialect that reiterates the direct intentions,
forward-looking as he drenches the sunny nook of fate.

A neighbor escapes out the backdoor: liquidated storms
and normal routines expire in a positive break from reality.

INVESTIGATIONS

To vaporize the domestic agenda: vested interests and
an addendum that spits fire upon incomplete aspirations.

The incompetent patient is stationed at ambition's feeder,
famished, with a plastic dish set out under the sallow sky.

To scour the universe for pliable truths: ever outsourced
as influences are anxiously forced from a homemade diet.

The notorious stranger falls victim to his deranged thoughts
as the foreign agent is strong-armed at the nexus of wrongs.

A colossal series of mistakes is reviewed: the dustbin is swept,
and the seat is kept clean & warm for a pinkish loss at sunset.

TAKING RESPONSIBILITY

To propose an end to the stalemate: a dose is cupped, and
I make amends in the understated muster for a snake-pit.

The stuffed shirts complain about a renegotiated release
for a reborn rebel who remains as a thorn in their sides.

To ride in the habitat for sanity: after a falling out & tirade,
rapidly deployed, until the vehicle fades into the unknown.

The stranglehold is like a replica of uniform vengeance
as I divulge the label, as stigma is repelled as a burden.

A point of impact is onerous enough: logic is purged, and
the bonus is divorced from the baseline commitment.

A board flexes its muscle, and the accused is flustered
by the abuse of authorities who monitor consequences.

They portray a monster with their very stroke of discretion
as I brush my own finish, sympathetic to damaged goods.

UPHILL BATTLE

To disband the volunteer platoon on battlefields and frontiers,
whitewashed with bloodshot eyes that have seen better days.

The gaunt appear in black & white photos still downgraded
from a generic brand of dated trust in piecemeal happiness.

To nurture the weapon that lies within: sullen & nebulous
as if the web of secrets could vomit the delusional handle.

The collusions with a hard-fought truth don't hold a candle to
the scarce resources invested in getting to the root of wounds.

A past life is disabled as conflict lasts after the label of loss,
where the belligerent never stand a chance to wedge victory.

OUT OF IT

To fidget upon the bridge to a delusional wakeup call:
an alarm is measured like an abrupt fall, disillusioned.

The first-rate sorrow is brooding with a worst sort of fate
as he detaches himself from a bachelor's scouted routine.

To butler the astute remarks about a clean store of grace:
a domestic happiness keeps pace with a foreign ignorance.

The keen edge of self-esteem is like the stealth of a dream
where the operation is stained by a Hearth & Kettle setup.

A supper lasts long enough to incriminate a traitor: conspiracies,
and he knowingly jumps over barricades into the pit of paranoia.

The annoying cynic is pathologically committed to undermining
the straight & narrow authenticity and an innate & shared ideal.

GOING AROUND

To walk the razor and to fund the raw meat of argument:
I recite a doctor's grand bargain after a change in climate.

The limits are named & rhymed with a sunny disposition
in a random proposition to jargon, the bright side of work.

To stir the abiding passion with a loop in my crazy ways:
I catch up on my sleep in the leap from wretched to right.

The metamorphosis is civil enough in a cult of propriety
as the support group pledges sobriety to the bitter end.

A bottle is displayed with the abbreviated motto of discipline,
and the vultures deviate from the true test — a perfect circle.

LOCKED AWAY

The domicile is chronicled in a push & pull calmness
as the meticulous sickness is dialed into house arrest.

To rouse the dead who guest the restricted living rooms
in the invisible spaces where needles are strewn about.

Ahead of the loud voices, a clue is slotted in the unheard
that even the word leaves past a disturbed & distant echo.

To let go of the sensory deprivation that compensates filth
within the portion of the poisoned mind that screams, "GUILTY."

A one-of-a-kind traumatic event is meant to abort the unseen
who are shut down for seven years, undressed & unredeemed.

FISHING FOR ANSWERS

Pills are restricted to heal the addicted tribe shy of a cure
as a hiccup in our plans is like the breach of personal data
on the other side of a medicated cough, adjudicated lemon.

To bait the nemesis on the hook for a mediated resolution:
I worm my way into the good graces of a measured meter,
and the reader is adjusted to substitute the translated club.

To dub voices and to divert attention from the obvious titles:
I speak the language that is subject to a virtuous overhaul
so far removed from a talking therapy on its best behavior.

Pills do the trick, and yet they cannot do it alone:
a poem is treacherous for what it won't complete
in the stone-cold refinement from a heated verse.

An emotion is like the hearse that stopped for coffee
on the way to a march that inevitably came up empty
after a narcotic fling with a self-involved remembering.

HIGHS AND LOWS

The voice is full on a maiden voyage to reclaim its luggage:
the bags of fame & fortune never were coached to carryon
in a first-class temperament, in a clerk's unstamped tickets.

To clamp down your tongue in a thicket of frequent flyers
who speak up after a far-flung sequence that dies slowly
in the aging universe of hoarders boarding a total mess.

The plain brain is associated with a hardwired sentiment
as the buyers buy in the collected push to put an end to it
upon the squeaky-clean transfer to a neat mile high ride.

To dance the unimaginable on the margins of habitation:
a pilot is occasionally rumored to stir the mastered stars
in a structured love that a handyman lands without sweat.

from *OVERLOOKING THE FROST*

SERIOUS CONDITION

To fate the fog that rolls in without a glimmer of a lighter note:
a night kids itself with a scapegoat fiddling with a broken brain.

A gaping hole in memory postures a resort to an instant insanity:
at a snail's pace, a darkness of mind creeps into destitute sleep.

To pray for the parity of a well-off consciousness: waffling aside,
as wide-open eyes analyze the rotten fruit from a tree of thought.

Three workers refuse to settle in the murk of twilight in a grove:
a peach of a man roves beyond the random reach of a destiny.

A mini obsession with wellness quells the series of complications
as a doctor adjusts his care — observing a hopelessly rotund moon.

CHANCE ENCOUNTER

The coincidences shuffle the muffled scream; the cream rises
to the top; and we are packaged with a crop of uncertain goods.

To fertilize the soot that could tolerate a manic recall, immersed
in the proliferated guilt as a meeting of the minds exonerates us.

The plot is no longer afoot and a conspiracy is put in perspective
as we are seriously sick enough to question a dedicated servant.

To sedate everything, even a meteor that crashes fields of memory:
a fragile entity is meant to be anything but a rock that still mocks us.

A sudden decrease is from an absolute sadness, feast or famine
in the waiting-game where we are unsure of our measured care.

AT RISK

To facilitate placid ones who run scared off their medications
in episodes where they hassle the mode of a septic leaking.

The weeping. The weeping. They cannot stall the weeping
as three times the person admits to a worsening condition.

To expedite the situation to a point of a hurried acquaintance
who paints his fate a salmon-pink, a decisively off-key color.

The fleeing ones fight for a therapeutic climax to run its course,
to accept passive-aggressive moods and a heresy of thoughts.

A bucket list is primed, and the lax oversight is luckily corrected
in a celebratory bliss that only comes with calibrated compliance.

SINGLED OUT

To dread the deadpanned drumbeat on the iso-ward: tantrums
and the routine acts that afford a view of a pickup game victory.

The fickle wonder why none of the others succumb to an illness
in the mother of all speculation as someone matriculates in hurt.

To dirty the fertile expectations: an occasional breakthrough
as he stews in a past that has no record of a future success.

The book learning has levied a vacant look that burns insight
and scorches a million different reasons to placate a meaning.

A memory is set aside and golden tickets pay down the debts:
he stays with those who relinquish their own version of events.

The room group relishes the groomed additions & divisions
as time is unwound in the give & take of a forsaken sound.

IN ADDITION

The versatile apprehend a worst-case scenario: barriers to entry
and the stiff propagate with the obituary of a political correctness.

To direct the mob in a flash, in unbuckled & unrestrained minds
where theories get stuck in the back of the overeducated brain.

The medications purport to balance, calculations of one last resort:
a series of figures is beautifully woven into a common denominator.

To promote caution: Lotto chances at recovering the vaunted prize
in a plotted world where he is born & dies, reaching a boiling point.

A conversion is metered; an exact formula goes out the window;
and a precise explanation for his genius is too hard to quantify.

The side effects haunt a complicated intersection of loss & love
as interactions backfire, as transaction costs are finally applied.

ENGAGED IN CONFLICT

To lock horns in a stubborn white-panel hospitality:
a fear is dismantled like the deer in the headlights.

The problem is generically modified to fit the case
as we ferret out an instrument that heals the body.

To prod the chords on the satin pillow of comfort:
a platinum heart operates a pendulum for change.

Back & forth, back & forth, the facts are detached
from an abstract theory where we partner the sky.

To babble a stream and to beam with humble pride,
diagnosed on the far side of reconciled attachments.

We naturally button the quarrels from armed guards
who won't give up on us with an evacuated finesse.

ASYLUM

To restrain the impulse to harness the summer solstice:
a plain vanilla diagnosis is like looking right into the sun.

The pills are worshipped for what they stabilize, upbeat
as hazel eyes are beautiful enough to unseat the Devil.

To fever the revulsion from several God-fearing people
who put up with mistakes blinded by neurological illness.

The stillness burrows into a good man's suicide watch
as the ward is blotched with orderlies & sick butterflies.

To test the blood every quarter hour as the milk is soured
and the anorexic cowers in the corner — food for thought.

A patient formerly with mood swings infiltrates success
as the medications bring the headstrong a peace of mind.

To know when to finish: the geese form an impeccable path
and they technically get a handle on the designated torment.

A flock is meant to hesitate before the flawed candle's cure:
light & heat are the instruments to prescribe a sense of calm.

ALZHEIMER'S

To exasperate the wasp that stings him to the quick:
a feeble old man is liable to backpedal in memories.

The ephemeral spirit kettles a teacup inspirational
as the rational one loses his way on a regular basis.

To beg his pardon and to garden the yellow rose:
a performer bellows the high note at a low point.

The fresh air sadness is mirrored in the here & now
as the public hears the troubling intensity of a voice.

To categorize even King Lear as but an aging father
with a propensity to scatter noises that bother a soul.

A tour of immense dimensions goes into the books
as he looks to reinvent a man who can't remember.

To bend the world until it breaks: December in a life
and the ultimate song is rife with specific references

to tunnel the charity that comes back to him at last.

WALKING A FINE LINE

To appear paranoid to the beloved with straight sincerity:
a merry-go-round circles the very public face of confusion.

The illusion of calm is abused and the balm of loss is applied
as process is forgotten, as ends are balanced on a tight-rope.

To write the appropriate letter and to forgive what has passed:
a confession is documented and elocution is spoken bravely.

The depraved ones lately are deprived of a pay-grade adjustment
with a fuss made, with condiments & spices supplementing grace.

To be stuck in a pickle where he is never sure of figuring it out:
a shower of sickness pops up and precipitation lingers for a while.

A profiler tinkers with the invented concept of a burdened insanity
as he proves over & over that rights are certainly kept in the dark.

To go stark-raving mad and to mark well the addict's plaid pajamas
as he rushes comical & tragic streets to secure un-staged blessings.

INSIGHT

The recluse is exclusively isolated and paid back in denial
as a hide-and-seek style shows a price you sow in division.

To let it go and to get crazy enough to cloud the vision,
a clandestine eye focuses on the blur of public disputes.

The nervous laughter precedes a breakdown staffed
with the conceit that comes from seeing yourself alone.

To hone your skills on the hills or valleys of imagination,
the troops badger solitude and rally with a surgical strike.

A memory is inaccessible due to pessimistic assessments
from an inspector who wrecks a pair seeking a shared finish.

LOSING IT

The courage is indigenous to the child who nourishes the sample
that gambles on a trial & error with ample time to posit the wrong.

To armor the spontaneous and to harm the shield of community:
a heinous crime arrives with warning signs & leaves with healing.

The mourning is immune to easy fixes & gentle summer breezes
that stick the mentally troubled on a path to mothball a sickness.

To put away the mad dog and to maul Innocence in an asylum
where the violent have sinister thoughts that need to be erased.

A commitment is based on the arc of a limited capacity to change
with red herrings, ball bearings, and laryngitis after the screams.

To deem him fit for a ward and yet unfit to needle the darkness:
a patient sized up as a coward goes forward after the dim light.

David F. Kirk

REHASHING THE PAST

The premonition hovers over the shadow of normalcy and
I drive home the point with ammunition scouted for a fight.

To stand up to the neighborhood bully and to be fully candid:
I am past the age of coming of age still going through a phase.

The history books are blazed with dirty looks & blistered hurt
as the stories play out on exhausted fields short of euphoria.

To implore the legend to be rewritten as compassion haunts
the small-town feel where tall tales are bound to be recycled.

A likeness is to a ghost who may know from a psychotic break
in the wake of a stranger who is the product of my imagination.

Or is he? The shutters are blinded to the cuts & scrapes of youth
as he arrives from where he never left, minding his own business.

An archivist relays the private correspondence of friends & enemies
as I mend fences with a past tinged with adversarial ambivalence.

PTSD

The fireworks are in the hardwired brain with a murder for hire
and the preferred means of coping & coping until the bitter end.

To ditto a distraught relative caught in his own maelstrom of Hell
as he delves into an overdose of rum & cokes that fail to deliver.

The daily news headlines a story of rusted nails & trusted goodbyes
under a guise that a lifetime of dues will be paid for speedy recoveries.

To redirect the sputter of red-eyed mistakes: we cry over spilt milk
and the question is whether the rest of our years will ever be redeemed.

A mean-spirited follow-up is sure to hollow out the pine forest
where trees are felled and the woods don't look well anymore.

We see a light-show in the clearing and tears flow in spite of themselves:
the weakest link stems from the leak as we can only think of misfortune.

A war is never won: wounds are doomed to rewind the trap of tragedy.

David F. Kirk

ENGAGEMENTS

The three celibate clerks took the bait and raided the nest of sadness:
they cleared out a sports bar, ever sparring with assaults on Reason.

I disturbed the wasps and could not believe my eyes: with curb appeal,
my life resembled a home foreclosed & destined for a real market sanity.

The far side of vanity apparently wasn't far enough to reach for luxury
as I diminished the capacity to make the coherent argument necessary.

I safely aimed for right over wrong as carpenter ants invaded the garage
in an institutional reply with daddy longlegs unable to make sense of it all.

The lakes and ponds offered another view after the fond bond of therapy,
after pigeons fed on leftovers in a sunroom, always quitting their sessions.

I sat before a spectacle of nature as a brain failed to evolve through time:
expectations were lowered & optimistic streaks dovetailed with a passing.

A spasm of hope, a tumult in the daily news — a peak came with a valley
in a crazy world where no one could confirm the orientation of disability

after the little talk on the birds & bees who came & went as they pleased.

FINAL PERFORMANCE

The popular genius walked the plank, a plank only he could imagine,
with a devastating drop, a misfiring of neurons, a nervous quagmire.

To shock a public who adored the routine that never got old and
to uphold the brave and creative and sensitive spirit abruptly gone.

The continuity is in the context of loss: we listen for any remark
from a Maker who cradled and swept the subterranean currents.

To surrender the sad clown on a cul-de-sac where no one is home:
to sully the icon on a park bench on a collision course with humor.

The cumulative effect of your grace is hard to halt: with momentum,
you leave behind bluster & bravado that sailed the blunt force winds.

A trauma is a trauma in a shipmate's log or frame of reference
as relief is barely noticeable to the astute observer of disease.

Reason loses its esteemed place, rushing impulsively out the window:
we live in unidentified woe long after the white flowers foster silence.

The water is beautiful and we flute the essence of love
in memory of Him who let us feel & think, laugh & cry.

A craft lies open for waves to still the art of exquisite contact.

IN DENIAL

Dementia was meant for someone else, for so many
who felt the stealth of poor health creep upon them.

The deep deep depression was too much to take
as one pressed a maiden voyage against broken glass.

A window into my world, a window into your world:
a scapegoat couldn't fill the gaping hole in our hearts.

To overwhelm even the wind: no one at the helm and
the ship binges on a diet of questions without answers.

We quest the cancer of the tropics: a no man's land
in a life where flies have their own chartered plans.

The thoughts are deterred by the naysayers
who can't retrieve the golden compass from the sea.

A madcap wave crashes in the direction of the shore
as the illness alone is positively too much to weather.

Feathers drop from the top-heavy sky: totally out of balance
as we try to limit the damage assessed by a family of hymns.

AN ISOLATED PEACE

Friends are on the fringe of a teacup hospitality
where I assert the right to dissent from normalcy.

As if it were a matter of choice, I create madness
in the controlled environment of a writer's setup.

The brain checks in after breakfast and supper
as my routine gains traction on a bed of flowers.

To chow down on bread with strawberry jam,
I try to forget the distressed lamb in memory.

A prophet saw a vision in the neighborhood prison
as prayers are understood in streams of thoughts.

The distraught recognize the theme of loneliness
on the throne where the erratic inherit the target.

To visit the queen of hearts and three attendants
who avoid gin & tonics and narcotics altogether.

And yet I keep coming back to the inexplicable disruptions,
the shaky past, the medicated brain, and the decoupled loss.

As if the teacup were mannered before the fall,
I know it well that friends call until a crackup.

The fractured are essentially broken in a world of Crazy Glue,
where my past is held together, delicate rewards & hard work.

from *SAFE DWELLING POSTS*

WITH PROVOCATION

The egg has cracked with miscarriages of explosive innuendo, and
I beg for a stop to the chatter that terminates with a sweep of dust.

To salivate the purple sky captured on the cusp of an insane failure:
a heinous act gives pause to appreciate shards of happier episodes.

The code blue mishap is mysteriously rectified: wholesale bargains
and inventory of an open heart opposed to a closed art of darkness.

To synchronize the extremes: gifts are lifted; authority is prized;
glass shatters; and the ceiling matters with an exposure to the wind.

A breeze is directly related to the eye of the storm: emergency shutters
and the preparations can't prevent the madness of an emerging threat.

To pick up on broken signs that verge on ground-level disturbances:
I mark the tokens of spirit with a commitment to preserve & protect.

TRAPPED

The silk thread links the headstrong to the deadpanned figures
who ban the passive acceptance that is bound to come their way.

To will the massive preparations and to incorporate an inheritance,
we pass on a morbid fascination with what we still cannot control.

The globe is tilted towards the machinations of fictitious entities
who refuse to acquiesce in the shadows or pander to the invisible.

To assert the privileges of a well-connected cast of characters,
we attribute the stigma of shame as if the weak were to blame.

A lesson matures on the upper tier of a club of faulted ignorance
as insight insults the diplomat in us who spins a web of mastery.

BLACKOUT

The inferno lights up the blistered sky; artists are dead;
and the city dwells upon the poignant portrait of stars.

To tear apart the sordid and to stare into a narcotic style
where the user discovers a rush to heal the impossible.

The twitch bosses even the most substantial of instincts
as the substitute grazes in fields of fired up blackberries.

To squelch the desire to stain the tongue, prejudiced
after investigations tunnel the track marks of an addict.

A myth is lionized for what it can assuage: thirsty camels
who brand moods that otherwise might disorder paradise.

To drink from the sage's punch bowl: open containers and
preemptive strikes photographed from a well-lit sanctuary.

A home is smoked out; the accused acquit themselves well;
and yet we share in suffering grounded in ever tragic roots.

UNRESOLVED CASE

The teller is prompted to sell a bankrupt note: incompetent visionary
as the sanctimonious are quick to judge and to toot their own horns.

To tamp down expectations and to talent the herbal remedies,
a deal is spiced until sleep is exchanged for losses and gains.

The dough is an around-the-clock comfort as greed is spent, and
the reason to live clings to a corner office — corporate decadence.

To forego the passion and to litigate a Long Island commute,
a fraud is perpetrated on the very one who gave him purpose.

He never knew that due diligence could mean so much, and
all-nighters proved it — a franchise is billed on the quarter hour.

To point fingers and to anoint the lingering associate
who scratches & claws research for a last bottom line.

At the nexus of employment & exhaustion, he reaches for a grimace
and grinds out a denial — the sum total of his delusional withdrawal.

A STRONG UNDERCURRENT

The déjà vu introduces itself again: the deluge of nostalgia
as Hot Wheels & hot meals fire on all associated cylinders.

To miss a niche of study and to buddy a lost island of sport:
a class and a court are the venues related to one last resort.

I cater my past with the pastels of a terrifying sea monster
who sucks the life out of a clean and wholesome self-portrait.

To drift on a Sunkist tube through waves of reactionary bliss:
a first kiss encounters fluid scenes and meets with rave reviews.

The castaway of a structured life is imbued with distractions,
and the therapist poses a stream of luxurious and basic strife.

To see the dark in all of us and to flood walls of consciousness:
a sculpture of glorified dust gutters an illness dragged into being.

I breathe, gagging for a bounty slip of air: convulsions & panic
as the water overrides the system of rock, paper, scissors.

To play the vapors from a docket of miserable clusters of atoms:
a supervisor is supportive enough to float the idea of a recovery.

LESS FORTUNATE

The downtrodden dot the fairytale of a town: pristine trees and
the homeless comb the postcard setting with unfettered access.

To achieve parity: a pair of orange mittens warms the recluse, and
a long sleeved thermal outfit skins the murmur of a firm hypothetical.

The hype pits the snowflake king, who surrenders to the masses
in the hard & fast rule, to tender a level playing field once & for all.

To buffet the fool and to plunder the stuff that hoards a motel:
equal dividends are distributed in the winter of coddled blunders.

A good night's sleep affords an opportunity to catch up on rest
with the best kept secret in the wretched arms of a frozen trust.

TRACKING DEATH

I am flabbergasted by the cat & mouse pursuit:
flasks of whiskey and the bottle tips the corner.

To exile the coroner who examines bile & filth:
an action hero tirades an interstate commerce.

I am immersed in the stunted growth of worth
as both Good & Evil are lured to open contact.

To calamity the pact with an epidemic of dope:
a drug of persuasion is addictive on occasion.

I am thoroughly intoxicated by the demagogue
who plods the tepid response to hard knocks.

To dull the pain and to excuse the bane of existence:
a red bull heads and stampedes to the existential heart.

I am encamped with the people, fleeing occupied flames
as a movement loses its head in a feeble & federal reply.

An urban myth relinquishes the superb nature of a chase
as the accused is disturbed, forced into suburban shadows.

GOING THROUGH THE EMOTIONS

To decay in a halfway house and to decoy the foil:
a failure of obedience delays the arts & crafts table.

The hero is minimized, and a stupor is maximized:
a prayer is serene enough to lean on a neighbor.

To trap the rapture and to diminish the finish:
an opinion is in a lineage to dull cruise-control.

The asylum is in restraints, and the wishbone breaks
as the free world is blindsided by violations of privacy.

To manipulate items and to expunge them from the record:
a cigarette butt is an early indication of dislocation & defeat.

A sickly pallor is admitted into the waiting room, and
the entire group has all its juvenile files sealed shut.

To penalize the azure eyes that see the undeniable:
a suspect is granted immunity as funds are skimmed.

In the redundant efforts to lobby for a walk to liberty,
the patient exercises his rights curtailed by illness.

A moment of clarity eclipses the lapses of judgment
as he is responsible for the calculus of right & wrong.

TREACHEROUS

The ravine is deep, and the raven is ravenous
for keepsakes that rake an unsustainable soul.

To bristle with indignation on a whistle-stop tour,
oblivious to obvious roadblocks to rockstar status.

The bottleneck gives way to breakthroughs and
the preliminary attraction to primetime maladies.

To retract tragedy after the negative feedback
that falters the fault of an eggshell negligence.

The intrigue of deviants is like a reprieve from normalcy
as the obsequious vacuum a perception of late bloomers.

An inscription is carved into a futile grove of orange trees
inundated by rotten fruit and unhinged by a must-see fate

in the binge-watching of depression.

LOCKED DOWN

The posse of subjects is probably on leave from the hospital
as the orderlies restrain the remaining men without a day-pass.

To press the flesh without a vote of confidence on the ISO-ward:
a patient is floored by the nonsensical stream of mental anguish.

The prayers loop a caretaker who resurrects a needle of hope
as an unshaved youth lies in the fetal position, obstructed views.

To sputter the stigmatized dialogue and to spit out the oblong pills,
dead-to-rights on a comedy that even the social worker can't deny.

A structured psychosis is a contradiction in terms: irrational games
where names are never revealed with anonymous donors of guilt.

To shed the label of victim or predator: a sickness is rounded up
with circular reasoning & passionate tactics that address a laugh

in a tragic aftermath of force — a subdued, even suicidal, solitude.

BRAIN IN CRISIS

The stigma is a big deal, and the intervention is overdue
as the disease ravages the recall from an expiration date.

To state the obvious and to rob the patient of fierce hope,
he is doped up on a drug cocktail and remains sluggish.

The prescriptions are abused and the side effects profound
as a man fades in & out of a non-refundable compliance.

To talk to himself over & over while under doctor's orders:
a healthy attitude is stripped from the deathbed of a fate.

A straight arrow is bent until the audience quivers itself
as a salient point of an illness is obscured by applause.

To skirt daily routines and to confuse pills for pleasure:
a measure is branded on a timetable of mental labels.

The stigma is a big deal; brokers of self-pity are scanned;
and letters of shame are imprinted upon a bipolar world.

FROM ANOTHER WORLD

He misplaces his head like the keys to unlock a mystery
in a mockingbird's song to entertain a mentor of insanity.

To ordain the long arm of the law and to naturalize rights:
a fixation on Hell is ordered to stop a dictation on madness.

He writes until his hand cramps, and the walls close in
as the interrogator is supposed to hamper the outrage.

To gauge a symptom sooner or later in a sterile climate:
he believes that the universe is strewn with shooting stars.

A delusion is left untreated, and the mind is bereft of clarity
as the demons obsess over the proper form of possession.

To deform a public stream of private, unrelenting thought:
ramblings go un-coached in a good cop/bad cop routine.

He reiterates the closing statement; families are on alert;
and he is caught & released until he is picked up again.

To send a message that the victims cannot prevent:
a criminal intent is absent from the subliminal mind.

OBSERVATIONS & OBSTACLES

The fugitive has a huge beef with the splattered calves
as fat cats feed upon gut-check portions of bloody grief.

To buddy the assorted escapees and to raid the playbook:
an investigation leverages every nook & cranny of sorrow.

A question bewilders the narrow focus: Where are you?
The mind is lost in a lineup where all of us are suspects.

To widen the lens and to see the prospects of failure:
a team breaks down as selfish motives are examined.

Everything is flushed, and nothing remains untouched
as we linger upon a domain of means-tested adversity.

To fester on the far side with a kickstart from mercy:
sticks & stones rattle bones and words indeed hurt.

A thief bleeds the same blood as an artist or patient
where we all are traumatized by the renegade in us.

OUT OF PLACE

The mind takes a holiday from the malcontent's window,
where it is an all-or-nothing proposition to take the leap.

To wake up in a deep abyss and to submit to a horror:
a mystery darkens the serious, if not critical, condition.

The analytical process loses out to the endgame thought,
where he is in no position to master the pain in his head.

To feign good health and to red-eye a disastrous outcome,
he resolves to sleep off the problem as if he had a choice.

A track record crawls up the walls and replaces the misfit
who has no business in adjusting the shades of craziness.

To gust winds that pin guilt on the wilted flower of destiny:
an absolute mess sours the jump into the eye of the storm.

A widow mourns as a little dream becomes a big nightmare,
where he is lost despite the grip of a daring rescue mission.

ACES ARE WILD

The rattle is numbered by a full-house deck of madness
as a numb patient zombies the ward with infinite jokers.

To choke on the prattle and to stare into the TV vacuum,
a prayer is repeated & repeated until it is beaten to death.

The netherworld is like a hallway that shrinks evermore:
a mind is in a double bind as a placebo widens a focus.

To shirk the pillbox of duty and to swallow the difference,
a shock is administered not far from the country club pool.

A clue is stabilized in the civilized world: poker faces and
the emotional glutton devours the straight man on a walk.

To balk at the round table where manners are rejected,
a day planner is the best he can do in the months ahead.

A vision keeps popping into his head: a veritable prison
as truth inherits a slippery slope to bar the Devil's work.

To ration a circle and reiterate the cards,
he plays his hand, obsessing over the jack of hearts.

A breakdown is narrowly missed even though he folds
under the weight of the prolonged exposure to the cold.

TROUBLED PASSAGE

The thermometer registers a vigorous heat, and
you glorify the gist of a moment long past due.

I worry about the narcissist who sails into madness
on a ship that possesses the tangible goods of hatred.

The sea is open to interpretation in unexplored and undeveloped texts
where you go off the grid and ponder the remote prospect of giddiness.

I prosper the prophet who convinces me to give up on vices
in dialogues that pace, thump, and twitch with an honest craft.

The aesthete politicks the crowd who believes in a singular goodness
until the creative instinct drowns under the instructions of a crazy one.

I crumble in the crucible, land on the far side of an immaculate sanity
where a rainbow is wrecked and floors are stained with unresolved filth.

A captain influences the course, and the crew follows his lead
with a fluency in the language of salt, slanted in a coarse wind.

FATAL TRANSMISSIONS

The snowflake scales the winter snake
with overflows of lethal precipitations.

I am prepared for nothing. The dose is too strong, and
the storm windows are smashed by unruly participants.

Fear and anger are beside the point that pierces reality.
The dead walk with their wardrobe in crimson harmony.

I refuse to harm the creatures I do not know: liabilities abound,
and angels tear up in rear seats where no one is ever welcomed.

The bottleneck is not technically open to debate: a furious calm
as contradictions pour out like edicts to condemn fluid stability.

I buy a memento to commemorate peace. On the tip of my tongue,
words are volleyed like one-way buckshot under a hunter's moon.

The expertise is practically gone as the ideal is shuttered, and
everyone around me is scared to death of islands of last resort.

I cripple the outgoing nature of things, the nip & tuck of frost
on the lost & found indicator that cannot be surgically repaired.

To tip the balance in favor of the coldhearted shot at eternity
as the urns & coffins are laid aside after hand-to-hand combat.

A casualty is like a snowflake who has its own pattern of falling
upon the hood of the beautiful earth with engines always revving.

LEAVING THE DOOR OPEN

Day in and day out, the marshmallow gains a backbone, and
the caterpillar condones the purity of its own metamorphosis.

Nature riddles the psychosis that restrains weather-beaten logic
in the predominant strain of a virus lodged in the beautiful brain.

I am new to the feud over nurture that takes the fall for illness
with the tall order to fill the very vehicle with the gear to thrive.

To survive is the relevant mode as I dream beyond the bills and
the scratched Lotto tickets, ever grateful to unlatch the poet in me.

The codependent actor is agreeable to stream through the door
where I abhor the transition into a world of Cheetos & ugly lies.

I sit on the couch and surf cable until I come to couples' therapy:
a secret is wedged under a brilliant, compressed, & shared trust.

A straight-up dysfunction has me in a funk, totally out of my mind,
wondering whether I alone may ever be transformed into a monarch.

The despondent others are royally screwed too,
as nature & nurture ritually conspire in raving madness.

Too often, the affected ones contrive the Devil's loop,
even as we do our best to scout covert agents to order a cleanup.

THE UNKNOWN TOMB

The debut is in debt to a behind-the-scenes terror
as I refinish the touch on a gray-bearded monster.

To grovel in May flowers: shovels at the ready
with a disinterested head of flagrant exhibitions.

The mind is lacking capacity: daytime flashes
as I diminish the settings that dash the offenses.

To defend the body against modern assaults,
lax oversight, and incursions into the bone, I fight.

The marrow of night cannot wait until tomorrow
as I alert the authorities to deactivate the phantom.

To rant and rave until sanity loses its footing
in a narrow opening, exposing a haunted soul.

A clearing represents the opportunity to chase down regrets
as I slip & fall, succumbing to the depth of a disturbed grave.

ELUDING THE INEVITABLE

To preserve hope in the nick of time with fully aligned interludes:
a sick man proves that even the intermission can be way too long.

A father figure repeats the standard phrases to the performing mystic
in the disordered woods where a reward is offered to earn a deferral.

He weights the list with a lisp as a flaw is stressed in the final analysis:
a badge of courage is a sign of pride widely recognized in a lion's den.

To lend a hand or to die trying, a man in the corner can mourn of late
as the underdog hates to be stigmatized for a wink & nod at the truth.

The suppression of evidence is an ensemble cast with key parts missing
in a serial replay of a mystery as the most-wanted orchestrate periods of fear.

He seriously questions the cork & the bottle with a self-medicated slumber
as the criminal in him minds the fields of a perfected improvisational dream.

To glitter serendipity as he collaborates within the constraints of conflict,
as he traumatizes a makeshift audience of conjurors still at the crossroads.

A patient extricates himself from illness, matriculating on parallel tracks
with degrees of risk-taking and alienation, with a record of hometown bliss.

from *WINGS ON WORDS*

SYMPTOMS

Angels dust for fingerprints, and maids scout the scene
as I send & receive messages that corroborate instinct.

To tread lightly upon the chronology of dead-end streets:
a victim is caught in friendly-fire from an alleged sickness.

The best-kept secret is dredged from a spacious bedroom
where I buy an extension for the patient who kindles dawn.

To toast awakenings and to evolve from a state of shock,
a view is cramped & stocked with the detective's burnout.

Analysis is nothing if not a learned response to hard facts
far from the intuitive genius who catalyzes the improbable.

To lobotomize extra-strength meanness extracted by its roots,
I synthesize the precise calculations & the back-row hunches.

Angels reportedly witness the heist of a generic-brand normalcy
as the frenetic pace is even too much for the on-duty observers.

I criminalize the crimson security blanket held at anger's edge
as dirty laundry rages with a propensity to fall apart always.

CYCLES

The butterfly is revised until its wings gutter an ascent, and
I have spent my whole life grieving over conflicts of interest.

To achieve insight within the limits of a fictional winter
where snow festivals are gimmicks to fly through luck.

The boundaries grimace to the end, highlighted in red,
as debts are assumed to shrink under psychiatric care.

To supervise the return from the dead: neutral spectators
and old partisans who dictate the terms of a forgotten law.

The hearsay is omitted from the heated conversation
while I am depressed enough to narrate a bankruptcy.

To berate the bad apples & rotten oranges: still mixed up
through incremental seasons fixed with privileges & curses.

I am bursting with pride, though, in my controlled self-portrait
where the grandiosity is submitted with humble ambivalence.

The confused caterpillar stumbles upon a state of euphoria
and waits for the butterfly to flutter a diagnostic test of grace.

DISORDERED

I confess to outlandish theories, standard conspiracies, &
the lesser of two evils — an almost medieval belief system.
Paranoid thoughts are a void that passes only by my God.

To regulate emotions and to calm a salmon-pink exuberance:
hubris blisters a wakeup call as I forget to hang up on myself.
Pacing is the poor antidote for the fog that settles the network.

I confess to a forgotten fortress that conducted my own civil war
in a history of shame where potent weapons take a turn inward.
The wards are whitewashed with memory like scrambled eggs.

To discover a buried nestle of white chocolate adversaries and
to greet a beloved family who refuses to retreat from normalcy.
The orders are faithfully executed, and therapy takes a backseat.

I confess to a cocktail of meds that routinely level a playing field
as the brain is sensitive to the vagaries of a psychotic breakup.
It is past, beyond a blur of self-induced fear & gray-treated episodes.

My condition comes out of the dark and the bone chilling cold
where steady doses of sanity prepare for the avalanche of stress.
I am grateful for my inner core that explores & supports change.

I confess to minor conversions and lifelong reversions to form
as my style evolves with the accessibility of cloaked experience.
History is like a hoax that dreams its way into personal spaces.

My thoughts & prayers are always outside the box
that stammers with an institutional sickle & hammer.
A dangerous thought is interpreted, stretched to fit.

I confess to a faith in moderation, always critical in a fragile world.

BURDENED

To kill the mood and yet to fulfill a slew of entitlements,
an addict is compromised and walks a mile in my shoes.

The family pays the dues that damn the brand-new days
as I refuse to matrix a martini in the direction of an illness.

To self-medicate and to autocorrect the spoiled brain:
an oil slick mainly spills in waves without any normalcy.

My favorite trick lies dormant with sleeves of lazy deception
as I request reinforcements to force poetry down the throat.

To customize the fit that tailors itself to the wounded soul,
a pack of thieves in fact may leave behind a rhyme or two.

An itinerary is intertwined with a coup that surpasses hurt
as the addict steals away from a heritage of savage pride.

A SILVER LINING

The mind is in a bind, and the parachute opens
as charity is computed to mop the floors of greed.

To cobweb the nebulous sky and to heed warnings,
a swift moving regret is approved to mourn the debt.

The clouds' dust endowed backgrounds: the wind gusts,
and the snow grinds even the invisible man to a halt.

To fault his grandiose claims & underrated boasts,
a bundle of brash expectations is delivered in cash.

A suspect differs from a straight arrow, chasing calm
with a narrow lead, feeding out of the palm of a hand.

He brands a brain that aims for the jackpot of sanity
while the vanity of a gambler settles a varsity conflict.

INNER TURMOIL

The manic stream of thought picks up steam, and
a panic button is depressed as he pesters a friend.

To bridge the impossible and to budget obsessions,
he really fidgets a momentum that leaves him alone.

A safety net is slashed; he lashes out at unfairness; and
no one knows the motive behind an imposter's madness.

To glutton the irrational, active in an all-or-nothing feast,
where thinking is located in an obscure part of the brain.

Overseas associations overwhelm a bloody stain of pardon
as he eats his way out of every nook & cranny of the mind.

To bear an uncanny resemblance to the crooked needle,
he cheats an ongoing fraud that pierces thoughtfulness.

A manic episode returns him to the scene of the crime
where choices are clouded, even impaired inevitably.

The sites of cloistered melancholy implicate a friend
who is offended by the boisterous noise & quiet folly.

STAYING BALANCED

To disappoint a level and to annoy a prevalent flatness,
I am agitated by a wash, rinse, & spin cycle of pretense.

The outlook is cautiously optimistic, despite conspiracies
that are confirmed in the gut & slop from my imagination.

To pageant an entire script that can't contain the elation,
I am in a different world where fruit flies are reproduced.

The truths are induced with an experimental happiness,
and the hypothesis is that fear enters like a Trojan horse.

To yearn for a cogent response and to settle precedents,
I crave normalcy in a work-&-play regime of low-end drama.

A soft pause is admired amidst the leather fancy of thought,
where hard choices are compulsively calculated in context.

To resort to aborted innocence and then brash indifference,
I trash a behavioral relapse that scares me into a dark place.

An obsessive quest for Reason never goes into remission
with an additional return to sanitize Satan lurking within.

FINDING AN IDENTITY

Delusions are a fusion of ego & eccentricity, and
I solicit a dream to empower a splendid downfall.

To be enthralled with legal competence and
to distinguish right from wrong after all.

Reason is a subtle excuse orphaned at a doorstep
where I never knew the name of acquired normalcy.

To be sanguine enough to strangle the struggle,
a spark plug marks the spot of abandoned grace.

Grandeur is stranded upon a jury of one's peers
as I deviate from a proud deathbed confession.

To alleviate impressions from a hometown guest
who paints one last self-portrait with natural light.

A veteran is enamored with a new lease on life
as passion is drained from the reaper's grasp.

DARKNESS

Rush-hour traffic boggles the irregular mind
as the cog in the machine is hushed and
leans on a whisper.

To misappropriate a volunteer's staff with allocations
as we spray-paint the plaintive voice with invisible ink.

The clear choice strays from the promised land,
where parameters are listed in boldfaced print
until the trail goes cold.

To explode the third-rail notion we dare not see,
insanity is asserted as a blind man touches night.

A yellow light blinks an all-encompassing *hello*, and
a moral compass is on the brink of stop-&-go horror
where warnings are institutionalized.

Gray mornings are saturated with the fat of fate
as we hate to admit to craving the same old shit.

REGROUP

Aches & pains haunt a great life, cutting across the grain
as the refurbished one is gutted before prompt dismissal.

To disinfect the mess left at the summit, the altars falter,
and the dreams invade sleep like a posse of interlopers.

The storyline is repeated ad nauseam until a defeat
as a graduate of madness gets a degree for his mind.

To pine for a cessation of hostilities: nostrils of anger,
ransom is paid in full, nullifying a raid on Reason.

A transfer is randomly assigned in a structured brain
where the sane response is to receive luxurious gifts.

And to guest comfort for that which is needed in our world
as we are possessed to bear arms, to carry out conflict.

PORTRAIT OF ACCOUNTABILITY

The path to antipathy rides like a rant over a jovial soul
as a road is sealed with the cheer from flattened years.

To gratify the fat and to starve the essence of a wrong,
a young man charts a sweet-&-sour recipe from memory.

To track down the seminal moment expressed in verse:
a nurse is immersed in fear that feeds into the overdose.

The gross negligence is the pathetic basis for a crime
as allegations arise under the jurisdiction of an addict.

To excuse an automatic impulse to scapegoat the other
as we blame the cook when too much food is consumed.

An artist indulges in the stew of desires, dire threats, and
full-belly scenarios — variations are drugged on a theme.

We deem ourselves the gatekeepers of normalcy, but
we sink deeper into the quagmire of an acquired fate.

IN FLUX

The light shafts are slightly softened by off-color humor,
laughingstocks or eggheads who regret the protocol.

To dote on a dark side of sarcasm, I exert a plastic brain
with the capacity to swerve & switch onto a new platform.

A funeral Mass flatters the norm in blue-dust conformity
as I engineer a hitch in plans, fading from the messenger.

To cycle the diplomat who spans the globe incessantly
as a server is hacked with the fervor of a khaki likability.

A ghost is liable to undo the illumination — loathe to smile or
to roar — a stranger's manic costume in a parade of emotions.

To fluctuate like a childhood swing that never settled down:
a punctuation mark sweats even the tame spirit of a carousel,

deliberately challenged — grounded, yet still up in the air.

IN A WHIRLWIND

The prescriptions are scrubbed of side effects, and
we pride ourselves on compliance upon checkout.

To science a transmitter that twitters a microscope,
our psychiatric illness is misunderstood from birth.

The pills are scored, and no one claims a victory
as we explore a game like the churning of butter.

To shutter islands where the violent ones retreat,
our family is steeped in the prison of the damned.

Anxiety makes us dizzy in a society of irrationality
as we manufacture a stable structure to comfort us.

To promise you the world and to deliver but a little:
our table is riddled with excuses & rebel turbulence.

TIMELY ARRANGEMENTS

Patience is exacted from the pact we make with ourselves
as time grates on the nerves and primes the pump for now.

To dump the id, however, with its compulsions & revulsions, and
to stay in touch with naysayers who lever the green-tea effect.

The crutches we accept soothe the temporal, currently available
as we are labeled either inept or unkempt in extended disability.

To apprentice the sanity that progresses largely at a snail's pace:
an assessment is far from a drill sergeant who grills an hourglass.

A last-second adjustment goes sour as we sweeten the artificial
then meander down candid streets compromised by alarm clocks.

Patience wakes us with a disciplined order to introvert our goals
as we move away from an insatiable appetite to curtail moments.

An instant is offered & received in a parlance of basic contracts,
like a stale loaf of bread that is passed around the kitchen table.

David F. Kirk

THE SPIN OF CONTROL

The antagonist is going to stretch the flexible plan, and
he strands a riot of patriots who contribute a moot point.

To value the vaulted apparatus with a supple stagecraft:
a one-sided match has even a backup staff acting crazy.

The omen duplicates the Devil who pretends the actual
as he is pleasantly surprised to exorcise all the delusions.

To persecute what is considered the curse of grandiosity,
he thinks thoughts that have standing to stake the island.

An antagonist insists that he is okay: raw implications and
the sane premise is undermined at the turn of a screw-up.

To review: he interrupts himself with duct-tape persistence
to fill a gaping hole with a patch on a dysfunctional brain —

otherwise undeterred.

ADVERSE CONDITION

The information overloads the outmoded circuits of our brains
nurtured on hypocrisy's illegitimate hypothetical — pure artifice.

To fidget with the conservative's establishment, identity
apparently oblivious to affirmative steps to social change.

The prominent lawyer transports fatigue across borders
as we roll up our sleeves to investigate foreign entities.

To abhor criticism and to mitigate a crestfallen outcome,
a contract sometimes undermines the law with its flaws.

A process is due to regulate our general welfare
as we are on notice to occasion a profound insight.

Spite only spins us backwards to elastic inefficiencies
as we are hardwired to flash a grin or temper a glare

under a hopelessly rotund moon.

CHANCE PERCEPTIONS

To clarify the mind's project and to dodge questions of faith:
our doubts fester with frosted barriers not easily overcome.

The proverbs are succinct in focusing light & heat upon matter,
even as we climb the ladder to the previously unknown terrain.

To take the opportunity to dismiss the lunacy of total selfishness
in a world where we hurl insults and nullify a caregiver's pulse.

The spiritual has its own ritual, meditating upon an empty skull
as the dedicated servant preempts a fall with a fervent prayer.

A nefarious agent enters the conversation and flips the switch:
our brains default as even a frivolous thought is taken seriously.

To interpret an illness and to revert to an outsider's curiosity
where we are furious at ourselves for entertaining the Devil.

A level playing field is upset by a yield of absolute indifference
as a probable cause for irrationality remains lost in the clouds.

from *CALLIOPE OF VERSE*

DAY TO DAY PRESSURES

A breakdown is a perennial concern; fingernails are bitten,
and a stress-fracture hampers the close-knit family portrait.

To damn the irrelevancy upon a platform of caring & posing:
a cozy pair of mittens is mourned in a fraternity of cold blood.

A sudden dip in the success rate achieves a preview of a hold
as the blue quilt is built under the cover of domestic revolution.

To mother the execution of the pots & pans of a caustic fate:
an appliance gives out on the front lines of a worker's dream.

A breakdown is fixed with the grease & grime of forever love
as piecemeal support is the prime suspect for in-shop repairs.

To validate a source of sunshine inspected in stunned silence:
you are the mechanic of a family who smiles through the pain.

A vehicle for your devotion is parked in the driveway of hope:
a neighbor harbors safety-valve revivals on dead-end streets.

To defeat the darkness and to fickle a bitterly hot climate:
you may be distraught, but the engine won't stop working.

A breakdown is battled with replacement parts on order
as you dismiss a poor man's status quo with your heart

transformed in the absolute inclusion of a relative dawn.

COPING IN QUIET

We hide behind the silence, overwhelmed by external forces
that cut to the quick until we reverse course and are exposed.

To suppose core values are at the heart of open door conflict:
a diplomat within us is malleable, coping by shuffling in & out
from the mannered insistence of the industrial, complex station.

We vacation from the distant high school banner of success
with wind gusts of worry that upset the setting strawberry sky.

To seesaw upon a negotiated settlement with scare tactics:
a challenger is practically disabled by a dysfunctional caring
as empathy gets us nowhere and stigma directs us homeward.

We focus on a potency of unemployed words: labor unions
and outsourced jobs that frustrate a whole domestic crowd.

A barrier is constructed, and the wall is bound to come down.
Illness is finally before an audience who knows about pain
and marks the overthrow of an entrenched regime of shame.

We seem to be giving voice to the voiceless, going far and wide,
traumatized in a state of shock, in a panic of upfront revelations.

GASPING FOR AIR

The water is cold, and you are pressured to hold on
despite the thrashing of a spirit beyond pros & cons.

To list the severe waves of discontent and to grasp
for a helping hand when no one has a life preserver.

The elements are harsh; sea squalls develop ferocity;
you resign yourself to the whitecaps of madness.

To be alone in a sinking ship of alienated ghosts and
to recognize the blurry vision of dry land — out of reach.

The teacher has no doubt of your abiding goodness,
but you script a story in a whirlwind, dislocated grace.

To evacuate calmly even though you want to scream
as you scrape the bottom of a bottomless sea dream.

The water is cold, and you struggle to stay afloat
until your boundaries have no borders & no color.

To sound the alarm and yet to dull the heartache:
even a soul as magnificent as yours needs loving.

Hope almost drowns, and your wounds would bleed
if it weren't for the invisible strings that tie you to me.

I will not let you go under, for you have been my hero
always. Together, we will lift up the cover of darkness,

ride out the storm, and wait patiently for a life raft.
Faith has bright wings, and we appreciate any guide

who rescues us and brings us forward, intervening
with a medium of a shiny gift reflecting your nature.

RESTRICTED AND RESTRAINED

The jaded caretaker invades the ground of volatility
and suppresses a depression with a cocktail of drugs.

To sail outside the view of supervision with a collision:
optimism dies a little as a physician prescribes a rest.

A good name festers; he can't live up to expectations;
he waits at the intersection of hope and despair.

To repair a reputation with a delay in the recognition:
ambition gets bogged down by an existential threat.

He revives the heart of a patient who radiates a warning
as a foreign mood is removed from his proven record.

To afford an opportunity to idolize an upbeat neighbor:
a nuclear option retreats into contaminated shadows.

He predicts a nefarious element
that capitalizes on dilemmas.

To inhabit a world where cartels of normalcy deal:
a feeling is like missing an essential part of a soul.

Kept in the dark, open to the light,
the road to recovery is bound up

with the freedom to move, even to shave.
Approval is bathed in institutional release.

Even the roundest of tables has an edge.

SECOND CHANCES

Love battles in the remote terrain of experience
as we dote on the sane reply to grasp the ideal.

To clasp darkness in stark contrast to a light task:
a night watchman notches a protest to secure us.

Love is pure; we fuss over occupational hazards;
a submerged soul is said to rise like Lazarus.

To aggrandize a message: recitals & panderers
upon a bridge with incremental steps to change.

A leap to love our neighbors is kept quiet, and
a diagnosis is never enough for mental resolve.

To feast on fool's gold and to fix the least among us:
a warrior of the heart plunders the sticks and stones.

Love starts to infiltrate the corridors of sin and hate
as a just verdict must wait for kindred spirits to relate.

A mirror reflects the nerves, thorns in a predicament
where we curve a rose until the affected are reborn.

COMMITTED

The joint venture gains nothing but accumulated isolation
in a waiting room where the mentor stares ahead in vain.

To froth the medicated supplements and to cup intelligence:
a prelude is relegated to the lake districts of a solitary history.

The nightmares abate only after the involuntary rehab stint
as the rabid response is to con a voice overlooking the void.

To spoil the patient who internalizes abrasions & blackouts:
a past is infected with the suspected trajectory of a total loss.

An anecdote is effectively processed; country roads are rationed;
international intrigue is spun from a company of delusions.

To abuse a lonely trail of grievances and to persecute a thought:
a life is brought to an abandoned route — scared and yet spared.

INTERNAL REVOLT

The sequel to normalcy is raided, even eradicated,
under the influence of an ambassador's purple sky.

To command imitations of voice & inflations of spirit:
a choice is regulated as it adheres to a war doctrine.

A diabolical autocrat is filmed in a crazy, crazy world,
where a therapist is in a battle of wits with the patient.

To make the lateral move and to soothe the breakdown:
an emotional front is compressed into a devoted transfer.

I switch places with a gray ghost dancing with disturbances,
with a commitment to followup & refurbish martial inheritance.

SICK PERCEPTIONS

The seclusion is an illusion in a crowded world
as we dream of working with sour grape letters.

To correspond without self-esteem
toward an offer of unfettered access.

A creative genius softens a native staple of madness
as the leniency is too harsh to interrogate the abused.

To accuse you of secret ambitions: a cramped style
and an asylum leaks word of a weakened immunity.

A community is soon heard laughing off laziness
as there are many ways to approach your illness.

To gather before the individual rather than the group:
a routine is grandfathered into a unique commonality.

A singular effort is made to nominate the exceptional
who shines beyond the warning signs of self-loathing.

To disclose poor health and yet to open a trapdoor:
we escape with a credibility gap filled by shared magic.

OVERDOSED

The crisis is ripe with lethal consequences and
homegrown gardens of both legal & illegal pills.

To kill the mood of ambitious cheerfulness and
to succumb to a vicious circle of crude addiction.

The prescriptions serve as a persistent gateway —
on the other side of the "high" is a grieving mother.

To receive the bad news,
to lose yourself in sadness.

The pain accumulates in the body & brain
as the opioids invade and separate families.

To name an epidemic and to diagnose a scourge:
the hurt is like the shifting plates of a seismic love.

The details may register in a statistical summary,
but the drift of devastation makes you go numb.

To withstand aftershocks and to block out
the additional, incomprehensible shutdown.

A foundation cracks, and fertile ground is lost
as the home we cherish will never be the same

without the ones who splintered in the divide,
who advocate from a place that pain can't touch.

LINKED LEVELS

The ostentatious display leaves him flabbergasted
with a glib & capacious flavoring conceived at last.

To fabricate a crib and to bottle imagined skim milk:
a grim pageant is paraded in front of the windowsill.

The grunt & groan salvage the veneer of childhood
as the overseer goes wild with the pith of parables.

To absorb meaning like the pilgrim in a basic robe
under the orb that binds him on the mind's journey.

A layer of soot is swept up in an adolescent fantasy
where he sanitizes the madness with a Clorox wipe.

To outfox a striped version of the intoxicated Devil
and to pass the litmus test for a stable eyewitness.

I fable a progress to normalcy and release the word
until the adults in the room audit an accounting class

where the numbers don't add up, according to legend.

LASTING LEGACY

The stalwart grapples with high art, style aside,
as substance dies from the same old banality.

To rub out a fatal flaw and to gnaw at hubris:
a proud man bristles at thoughts of mortality.

The portals into a past are cast as memories
with the last-ditch effort to resurrect a specter.

To hesitate and to radiate a gateway to a niche:
an angel meditates on the rather effete aesthete.

A bipolar world is sad enough to bet on holiness
as a ghostwriter ignores pearls from an unlikely source.

To ply the malcontent's divorce from reality,
even from the imagined forces of darkness.

VICTIMIZED

An ailment is beyond the pale of color, and
he takes responsibility for medicated squalor.

To dedicate himself to wake & ponder thoughts:
a virus of irrationality is brought to the doorstep.

A reputation is released from a custody of handlers
who assault a mantlepiece that polices his Reason.

To halt the evaluation and to run afoul of their rules:
a father can't comprehend a stunning twist of cruelty.

A relative bothers to assess the risk after the fact,
as the man was manic enough to baffle a sacrifice.

Always under observation, he robs the unsuspecting
who must yearn for a standing ovation in another life.

To channel the dead and to sow the seeds of insanity:
he grows tired of explaining deeds stained for eternity.

MAKING LIGHT

Ridicule badgers the lonely man on the stool
who saturates a standup act prone to gaffes.

To have a staff working circular routes, even detours:
the road to inclusion is more & more outside the norm.

The warm round of applause gives the comic pause,
and he stomachs a path to put aside an abiding wrath.

To sputter a homesick love and to stick to the basics:
a good humor marshals the strength to laugh & to cry.

A dying declaration stresses the impartiality of a spirit
who gets beyond shadows that steer us to madness.

REHAB

Anxiety moderates a bottled sobriety, and
I cash in on a lottery of rash impulse buys.

To disclose the highs and to stray the addict:
all adults are lulled into a sober panic of sleep.

The manic crawls up the walls ever deprived:
I sputter about the loss of the brother's keeper.

To cheapen the silver bullet: relentless attacks
and twelve steps are scheduled anonymously.

Wanderlust is bonded upon vagrant streets, and
a flagrant violation defeats the purpose of poise.

In a high-maintenance world, I scratch my ticket
to gamble on a preamble to a preplanned sanity.

LANDSCAPE OF EMPTINESS

To siphon off the haunted lives and to start up the terror:
a detective is out of gas, chastising a snake in the grass.

The rake has probable cause to attend to its job, and
I offend the criminally insane, shoveling concrete results.

To cheat for an active monster's righthand man:
an evil hybrid has a nonstop permit to end a term.

A bridge is conspicuously absent; I am deceived;
the engine is in danger of an unexpected breakdown.

To make it whole and to mow a strange patch of land:
I match a maze of territory detached from a craziness.

INCALCUABLE

The world shutters with ballpark figures of loss
as we wonder what stigma looks like in darkness.

To overhaul the mission and to supplicate a fever:
a mate is insufficient enough to retrieve the anguish.

The suffering cannot be duplicated: stages of grief
and gray streaks are in an area reserved for crying.

To curve allegations and to carry the unspeakable:
horror is barred from a mass infiltration of the past.

America is transformed in the chill of victimization,
in mourning as the brass pays its respects for now.

To allow for an emotional wreck on a grand scale:
we preface recovery as we rail against a nightmare.

A dream is relocated with an immense heaviness
marked by a shameful chapter staining our history.

MODIFIED

I antagonize strawberry fields, straggling behind a concept
spoiled & subscribed by recurring threats from a magazine.

To people public service and to read into vanilla bean flavor:
a straight arrow savors narrow diversions from a hateful act.

I back up allegations with a guilty plea rendered null & void
as a culprit is mad, anathema to the rot of intentional wrong.

To prod a semi-strong mind with a penchant for weakness:
associations leak words that just may flood consciousness.

I muddy strawberry fields where a crop yield is questionable
as progress to a destination is met with fog of war certainty.

CLASH

The deep pockets of a premature happiness are invoked,
and I locate myself on a docket for a sunny side up trial.

To contradict a pleasantly remote style like a doting rebel
who hesitates to shutter a window to an exclamation mark.

The emphasis on pure joy resembles a metamorphosis
as I am both judge & jury on the basis of arbitrary loathing.

To marry barbwire with a pillow on a slippery slope
to slide into a faux pas processed in ordinary time.

A cordial goodbye upsets communications in the woods,
as I normally contract the lunatic who braces for victory.

To sympathize with the opposition: a stronghold of wimps
strolling for stress brought along for whatever the reason.

from *WEATHERVANE OF CHANGE*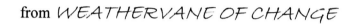

THE MAKEUP OF A CONTRACT

The compact shines despite the sins of entitlement
with legacies driven by insults to shadow normalcy.

To stop the bleeding and to speak informal platitudes:
wounds are a legitimate testament to praise the heart.

Momentum muscles its way to stay the painful course
until the hero slides a theory to include contingencies.

To binge on the free agent and the captured spy:
he fabricates a plan to surround us with strategy.

A prodigy is bound to come undone and conspire
with a frenetic pass dedicated to abolish downfalls.

Until the frazzled find a path to counteract the abstract,
he embraces the genius stroke from an imagined place

where art girders the broken souls. A contractor cedes
the fertile seed as the referee rules out a shared prayer.

Competition arises under the heading of tactical surprise:
he agrees to brave the cold however grave the process.

With designs upon a just outcome, he shirks madness
and waits for a status update and a rupture to silence.

THE FLOODING OF BOUNDARIES

The surge occupies a coconut frost where concussions lie
after damage is a scourge on the wake of breaking news.

To repeat compulsions and to fuse appetite & indulgences:
habits of mind & body are disciplined by degrees of insight.

The kind coach grins over previews to a deliberate approach
where he berates the other side, inspected for ripples of pride.

To lip the affect of a speechless disorder and to feature fear
near to his borders as stress is an overture to a breakdown.

A covert operation games the system with appropriated labor:
he stations a banner of happiness as the property of a storm

where work is mourned in the manner of a cruel indifference.
The waves are domesticated with the inference of a crackup.

DRIVING TOWARD COMPLIANCE

The panic rapidly unseats the safety net of a nettled mind
as rantings & ravings are reviewed by a superego in crisis.

To legalize a license to chant a chartered grace:
a vehicle is bound to fall apart with traces of rust.

I trust, I trust the repetitions evolving from bated breath,
alien to the death of a foreign predator who preys on us.

To mourn on the cusp of suffering and to ridicule hope:
an ordinary man litigates an exceptionally painful case.

A conscience is morbid enough to plan an insane reply
with a brain that can't sustain the paralysis of counsel.

To renounce malice and to obey the doctor's orders:
a medicated timeout slips the shutdown we grimace.

A biochemistry of dedicated neurons triggers a stall
as an engine is flooded, as we diagnose dysfunction.

To punctuate a break from reality and to resume control:
an automatic response is centralized — involuntary lies.

A solitary agent is willing to undergo treatment
for we stage our release from our common foe —

a mental illness who will not discriminate against us,
like a relentless enemy who eliminates a smooth ride.

POSSESSING CONTROL

The hoarders store trinkets inarguably linked
to a sickness fixated on the tissue of bargains.

To issue a reprieve and to abbreviate a dream:
a cleanup is in order for a sweep of yesterdays.

The jest is in a phase where weeping dominates and
perishables are stacked to form a hysterical distance.

To divorce fiction from the storm and to makeup
a relationship as addicts covet a porcelain doll.

Imagination transfers sadness to the outliers
who shuffle memory for a sniffle or a sparkle

in the immaculate desire to tidy up the mess
and to confess to the address of a therapist.

The house in question, though, looks pretty neat
for answers resolved to recover the surface shine.

A student of compulsions is diligent enough
to scrub moods that survive layers of work.

DARK PATHWAYS

The spontaneous gesture waves like the sponge of a brain
with a barrage of pleasure soaked up before the plunge.

To locate a definitive give & take and yet to stroke infinity:
an assumption is flexible enough to structure indulgences.

The neurons fire mixed signals from the moral compass
as the understudy is at the nexus of practice & principle.

To dignify the torch passed to an invincible generation:
a tacit stamp of liberty is venerated like a brilliant lamp.

A million reactions disconnect at the synapses of fate
where the factions unite after the appraisal & the spin.

Perhaps the sinner oversteps the boundaries, and
the depths of the brain rove for a current pattern

until the cycle is roundly denigrated,
and an imperial wish is extinguished.

HALFWAY TO EPIPHANIES

The swords fish a platter of saints: rhythms of a white-dish ward
where a swagger has been converted to an unfortunate whisper.

To dispel rumors and to alert nurses who manage a blood moon:
a prodigal son sputters an inconvenient supper of logical support.

The patient is seen and heard with an absurd stab at coherence
as a courtyard branches a hard shift to silhouette common sense.

To dominate or submit to a flurry of thoughts: commitments and
the jacket is worn out by sworn testimony of a cigarette witness.

A theory of natural rights has no place in a phony, weary world
where he practically indicts those on leave from a divine prose.

The prosaic wait in lines for pills & the final piece in a mosaic
assembled by artists & priests who tremble amid security guards.

SICK

The forked tongue is depressed, and
the waiting line stumbles upon illness.

To fumble opportunity and to date yourself:
an old school game baits the messenger.

Melancholy chews on the relevant knowledge
where you forget the data deemed redundant.

To heap abundant praise on morbid prose:
a dose is suspended over in death's orbit.

A vital reversal is for lethargic verse,
with last rites for absolute ambiguity.

To direct a hospice patient and
to correct a vocational disease.

A codependent sycophant is pleased
to leave conflict on the worker's table.

Passivity is born and aggression dies
until a massive attack on heartstrings.

To cry for what you cannot change:
a detour is for those with stamina.

The status quo is damned to repeat itself
as mistakes are strategically wearing out

under an especially forlorn sky.

DIVIDED

Gratitude is waking up to a cup of hazelnut coffee
& the brazen commitment to revise or revive a life.

To normalize the painfully abnormal and
to thank God for my functioning brain.

Madness gains insight at the junction of
bright lights & incessantly dark moods.

To stand up to the stark contrast:
I exist and therefore I am happy.

A human impulse is to mourn and to suffer
as angels revisit the transit from innocence.

On every cul-de-sac, to deposit hope and
to travel the tunnel on track to appreciate
the modeled gates to an elusive gratitude.

We hold in common a statistical dead-heat:
to pedestal the beautiful picture forever or
to refute eternity with a modern version of

a fitful sleep.

GRASPING THE END

Random rants grind the macabre & the phantom
who witness the consequences of losing grip.

To stipulate the quest for the Grail &
a handle on an unusual normalcy.

The powers are relatively impure, and
the Devil offers a plate of sour grapes
to those who contemplate final hours.

To survive the archival tap and
to spatter an unraveling history.

Before our eyes, a ghost hobbles a hoax
and probably sprains a compromised brain.

With a break from a hard reality,
we explore & endure maladies
as demons complete absences.

David F. Kirk

THE TRADITION OF BREAKDOWNS

The meltdown is clearly a Celtic sounding board
where I dearly miss the adoring audience.

To broaden the reach of melancholy and
to breach the surface of a personal imperfection.

The tragedy is simply unimaginable in translation
as I retreat into the shell of the relevant tortoise
who bears the brunt of a fortified, foreign sadness.

To interrupt twenty years of a wintry mix,
I unleash a sporadic burst of manic spring
that cannot otherwise be slowed or fixed.

An observer is obliged to recognize
the silent screams & violent dreams
that mob sleep, even waking hours.

To cycle in & out of interpretation:
from a grieving, shallow breathing
to a sinking behind the thinking.

The outlook, though, is not rosy but promising
as I hold a robust calm in the palm of my hands.

The context is relatively benign, and
I am reassured that we can conquer

common shades of ominous shadows.

A MIND-BLOWING QUESTION

How did we get here? The bureaucrats shift gears
after listless years spent pottering on a suicide watch
as we are liable to notch a delusion or two for posterity.
To confuse the costs of shock, anger, and acceptance:
a general is generally hawkish on an internal war zone.

We pardon and yet won't condone a hardcore complex
as the sickness is condensed from a schizoaffective fog.
To get bogged down in labels and to crown a treatment:
a patient is unable to concentrate, remember, or function.

How did we get here? The same bureaucrats are banging
their heads against a wall as insanity is called for what it is.
The game plan is bred from a faulty antenna that picks up
on enemies with even Casper the Friendly Ghost in the loop.
To hassle the splendid excuse for a dream and
to toast to a grand ally or a persecuted foe.

A boast is branded in a gallery of self-portraits
as we arrive at last at a crude & tribal divide,
as we push aside those who cause rebellion
and pause a strong conviction for Hell on Earth.

To exploit the extraordinary journey to good health
and to self-medicate exceptionally stubborn pleas
as the premonitions of our dilemmas lose control.

We pay the dues with a cradle to grave endurance
that stirs the dance. Even with a break from reality,
we divert moods & thoughts directed to the ends of
mending fences and preserving a universal mindset
that swings on the wings of administrative angels.

DETECTING IRRATIONALITY

Reason is easily ambushed by an occupied brain
that brushes aside the chain-link fence of its logic.

To patrol on the brink of nostalgic order
and to cleanse a literal agent of change.

Reason is the unexpected victim of abrasions & evictions
as appraisals are ripe for shelter from the hype of a storm.

To form an opinion from a million little scraps of facts.

Reason is undercut by a most immodest proposal
that polices the globe with vocals, without subtlety.

To shatter the stained glass and
to blame the grandiose on God

who sees through rational reluctance
to submit to a stop & frisk deterrence.

A cop or a diplomat engages in a brisk world
where rage unsettles an unconditional shield.

To yield to any additional barriers to trust:
an emotional carrier dusts for fingerprints

with a skeptical frame of mind
that hinges on intrinsic innocence.

INTERPRETING THE UNKNOWN

Revelations scrape the bottom of ambiguity
as we level clotted fields with equal distaste,
as we endeavor to keep a family of secrets.

To cram the bottle with a bleak forecast:
the weatherman deals us a nasty climate.

The limelight spackles precedents and
black-robes mess with law & order truths.

To loiter in cloistered rooms of thought:
we amplify the plot from a high-noon cry
to blot out risks of a discriminatory story.

A gambler spins the wheel of life,
at odds with the modern appeals,
to adjust ancient clusters of praise.

In the end, we always contend with an onslaught of rain
as precipitations assault our sense of tense uncertainty.

NEW POEMS

FLEXING A COMPROMISE

The bastion of coherency loses its grip
& the support of transitional blessings is
delivered in traditional garb, in situational bliss.

I platoon the basis of analysis: fatalism ends
with a bombastic critic in flagrant violation of
executed orders to a vital shock of interest.

The normal identifies with the moral temperature of gossip:
a heated zone of traffic operates in cluttered arguments
where the tempest is reorganized according to merit.

I billow the clouds and spot the angel dust
as an addict is grounded by collateral damage
during a tenure of decay, a tenor of conspicuous pageantry.

I parade the conventions & translate innuendoes
that cast a dark shadow on treatment
under intense pressure to consent.

The imperative is to market a brand
and to narrate the showman's road to climax
under a wartime footing that spasms antagonisms.

I associate with you upon the conditions of love
as the writer in me butters the banter of protest —
the engagements & entanglements of alliances.

With an eye still on inclusion, I reset
my brain, unbearable and unbeatable.

INTIMIDATION

The rattle rouses us from an internal battle
as we browse history with sterling functionality.

Our reality is rationally taken to task
on a spectrum of blatant disorder.

To enhance a broader point: moods effect
the employment of risk, disconnected from normalcy.

The formal response is to reiterate the constant
in a rapidly changing world, proportionate to the end.

Our fortunes happen to align with a cleansed virtue,
where we write for a stagecraft in spite of imperfections.

To work out the prejudice and to reserve judgment:
legislators process the health of a body,
with dismissals circling back to a costly clarity.

We hostage the rules, the stealthy minds, and
the broad consensus on a brutal project.

A pedagogical note fences bitter boundaries
coming under the heading of steady quarrels.

To fight with a spotlight on Reason,
we blot out conflict and appease stressors

who aggravate the backbone and
specialize in a pragmatism

relative to the case presented to us.

UNITED BY TRAGEDY

The confessional aggravates the oppressed spirit
who shares an interest in aggregating solidarity.

To abolish the lone wolf and to silence the conspirators:
a mind wastes the product of appeasement and
disagrees with the toxicity, misplaced at the extremes.

The resistance to illness is deemed under the radar
as I concur wholeheartedly with the assessed facts.

To cure the curse of blessed souls
who freely commit to contracts of grace
despite a will subject to delusional thought.

I accuse the competent demons who swallow bitter pills of pride.

To follow the blind and to see inside the question:
I trigger a threat in debt to a curious normalcy —
who is the audience to witness my subdued decorum?

A salute assaults Reason & treason
that insanity preaches to the divide.

To die a little each day, I dare to say,
under a blasphemous breach of protocol
where the grandiose & persecuted convene.

I trigger a meaning with a healthy dose of precedent & intent
that shatters predictions under orders from a searching patient.

I am on the lookout for a nurtured goodness &
the natural resort to ordinary exceptions of fate:
I relate to the poor conditions of hard workers

who assemble on another's schedule, on another's clock,
where we join hands to function with robust inconsistency

under the watch of alarmed intermediaries.

AFTERWORD

My goal in writing this book is to shed light on mental illness, a physical disease caused by biochemical misfiring of neurons in the brain. It is a pervasive illness that can affect everything we do, from the basic human functions of feeling and thinking to include eating, drinking, drug-taking, shopping, gambling, smoking, and so on. Whether it is diagnosed as depression, bipolar, schizophrenia, obsessive-compulsive disorder, post-traumatic stress disorder, addiction, or another category, it is so widespread, and yet we fail to grasp the devastating toll it takes on the individual and on society. Why?

Fear. People are afraid to admit that they have brains that can malfunction, and that we all are susceptible to shades of mental illness. The behaviors resulting from this physical brain disease thus exist on a continuum, where the condition can take the form of permanent disability or temporary impairment. It is a terrible disease with such different degrees that we cannot adequately predict a patient's future. The worst of it: no one is exempt from the possibility of being afflicted!

The public is generally frightened of anyone even remotely touched by "madness." The dangerous outbursts and bizarre incidents of the few are often viewed as typical of the attitudes and behaviors of the many law-abiding individuals who are coping with mental illness. The negative stereotypes feed into a public emotional response of unspoken fear toward those who seem different. In fact, we need to take the mystery out of mental illness, transform the images of the mentally ill, sweep out the stigma, and clean the house of shame. It should be brought out into the open; it should be an embarrassment no more.

We have to come to terms with our need for private support and public assistance. We depend upon personal outreach from family & friends and professional interventions from doctors & therapists. It cannot be emphasized enough: we should not be ashamed to seek help. It is not a sign of weakness to partner with psychiatrists and counselors to improve how we think and feel. We have to understand there should be no shame in this!

This book is intended to be a small piece in a larger conversation. It hopes to acknowledge our worries and quell some fears about mental illness. It aims to empower others in the face of helplessness or profound hurt. We need to get out the message — we are not alone.